RHUBARB REVELATIONS

A CULINARY HISTORY AND RECIPE COLLECTION

THE RHUBARB COOKBOOK

MASTERING COOKING TECHNIQUES AND STORAGE TIPS

Table of Contents

Rhubarb Revelations
A Culinary History and Recipe Collection

Chapter 1: The Origins of Rhubarb 8

    Ancient Beginnings: Rhubarb in Early Civilizations 8

    The Journey to Europe: Trade and Cultivation 10

    Rhubarb in America: Adoption and Adaptation 11

Chapter 2: Historical Cultivation Practices of Rhubarb 14

    Traditional Growing Techniques 14

    The Role of Rhubarb in Early Gardens 16

    Cultivation Challenges Through the Ages 17

Chapter 3: Rhubarb in Traditional Medicine: Folklore and Facts 20

    Medicinal Uses in Ancient Cultures 20

    Folklore and Myths Surrounding Rhubarb 21

    Modern Scientific Insights 23

Chapter 4: Regional Rhubarb Varieties and Their Unique Uses . 26

    Common Varieties and Their Characteristics 26

    Regional Specialties: From Yorkshire to the Americas 27

    Unique Uses in Local Cuisines 29

Chapter 5: Rhubarb in Literature and Art Throughout History. 32

Rhubarb as a Symbol in Literature... 32

Artistic Representations of Rhubarb 33

Rhubarb in Popular Culture 35

Chapter 6: The Evolution of Rhubarb Recipes in Different Cultures Historical Recipes and Their Transformations 38

Cultural Variations in Rhubarb Dishes 40

Modern Interpretations and Innovations 41

Chapter 7: Rhubarb Preservation Techniques: Canning and Freezing... 44

Methods of Preservation 44

Best Practices for Canning Rhubarb 46

Freezing Rhubarb: Tips and Tricks... 47

Chapter 8: Rhubarb as an Ingredient in Modern Gastronomy ... 49

Rhubarb in Contemporary Cuisine.. 49

Innovative Chefs and Their Rhubarb Creations 50

Rhubarb in Fine Dining.. 52

Chapter 9: The Role of Rhubarb in Seasonal Cooking and Festivals... 55

Rhubarb Harvesting Seasons 55

Festivals Celebrating Rhubarb 57

Seasonal Recipes Featuring Rhubarb.. 58

Chapter 10: Rhubarb Pairings: Exploring Complementary Flavors... 61

Sweet Pairings: Sugars and Spices 61

Savory Combinations: Meats and Vegetables 62

Beverage Pairings with Rhubarb 64

Chapter 11: The Impact of Climate on Rhubarb Growth and Culinary Uses 66

Climate Requirements for Optimal Growth 66

Regional Climate Variations and Their Effects 67

Adapting Rhubarb Cultivation to Climate Change 69

Chapter 12: Rhubarb Recipes: A Culinary Collection 72

Sweet Rhubarb Desserts 72

Savory Rhubarb Dishes 74

Preserved Rhubarb Delights 75

The Rhubarb Cookbook
Mastering Cooking Techniques and Storage Tips

Chapter 1: Introduction to Rhubarb 80

The History of Rhubarb 80

Nutritional Benefits of Rhubarb 82

Selecting and Storing Rhubarb 83

Chapter 2: Rhubarb Cooking Techniques 86

Preparing Rhubarb 86

Cooking Methods for Rhubarb 87

Pairing Rhubarb with Other Ingredients 89

Chapter 3: Rhubarb Recipes 91

Rhubarb Desserts 91

Rhubarb Pies 93

Rhubarb Crumbles 94

Rhubarb Cakes 96

Savory Rhubarb Dishes 97

Main Courses with Rhubarb 99

Side Dishes Featuring Rhubarb 101

Rhubarb Beverages 102

Cocktails 104

Smoothies 105

Teas 107

Chapter 4: Rhubarb Preserves and Jams 109

Techniques for Canning Rhubarb 109

Recipes for Rhubarb Preserves 110

Creative Uses for Rhubarb Spreads 112

Chapter 5: Gluten Free Rhubarb Recipes 115

Gluten Free Desserts with Rhubarb 115

Gluten Free Main Dishes Featuring Rhubarb 116

Snacks and Treats for Gluten Free Diets 118

Chapter 6: Rhubarb and Seasonal Produce Pairings 120

Spring Pairings: Rhubarb with Strawberries 120

Summer Pairings: Rhubarb with Berries 122

Fall and Winter Pairings: Rhubarb with Apples and Squash 123

Chapter 7: Rhubarb for Kids 126

Fun and Easy Rhubarb Desserts 126

Kid Friendly Savory Dishes 128

Engaging Kids in Rhubarb Cooking 129

Chapter 8: Rhubarb in International Cuisine 132

Indian Rhubarb Dishes 132

Scandinavian Rhubarb Recipes 133

Other Global Rhubarb Inspirations 135

Chapter 9: Rhubarb Health Benefits 137

Nutritional Profile of Rhubarb 137

Cooking with Health in Mind 138

Incorporating Rhubarb into a Balanced Diet 140

Chapter 10: Conclusion 142

Embracing Rhubarb in Everyday Cooking 142

Final Thoughts on Rhubarb Creativity 143

Encouragement for Home Cooks 145

Chapter 1:

The Origins of Rhubarb

Ancient Beginnings: Rhubarb in Early Civilizations

Ancient civilizations recognized rhubarb as a significant plant, not only for its culinary potential but also for its medicinal properties. The earliest recorded uses of rhubarb date back to ancient China, where it was cultivated as far back as 2700 BCE. Chinese herbalists valued the root of the rhubarb plant for its purgative qualities and used it extensively in traditional medicine. This early adoption highlights the dual role of rhubarb as both a food source and a medicinal herb. Its use spread along trade routes, making it a valuable commodity in early agricultural societies.

In ancient Rome, rhubarb gained prominence as a luxury item. Roman scholars documented its benefits, particularly the root, which was sought after for its therapeutic qualities. Pliny the Elder, a Roman naturalist, wrote about rhubarb in his encyclopedic work "Natural History," acknowledging its effectiveness in treating various ailments. The Romans' appreciation for rhubarb not only influenced its cultivation in Europe but also contributed to the plant's status as a symbol of sophistication in culinary practices. Recipes from this period often highlighted the tartness of rhubarb, incorporating it into dishes that balanced its sour notes with sweeter ingredients.

As rhubarb made its way through the Middle Ages, it became an integral part of European agriculture. Monastic gardens began to cultivate it alongside other herbs and vegetables, recognizing its value in both cooking and healing. During this time, rhubarb was often used in pies and tarts, establishing its reputation as a staple ingredient in sweet dishes. The preservation of rhubarb through drying and pickling became common practices, allowing people to enjoy its flavor long after the growing season had ended. This adaptability set the stage for rhubarb's enduring presence in the culinary traditions of various regions.

In addition to its culinary uses, rhubarb was steeped in folklore and traditional medicine throughout history. Many cultures believed in the plant's magical properties, associating it with various rituals and remedies. For instance, in some European communities, it was thought to ward off evil spirits when hung above doorways. These beliefs reflected the intertwining of food and culture, demonstrating how rhubarb transcended mere sustenance to become part of the social fabric of early civilizations. Traditional recipes often included rhubarb not just for its flavor but also for its perceived protective qualities.

The evolution of rhubarb in different cultures showcases its remarkable adaptability and significance. As trade expanded and culinary practices evolved, regional varieties of rhubarb emerged, each with unique flavors and uses. From tart varieties favored in English desserts to sweeter cultivars embraced in North American cuisine, rhubarb has been celebrated in diverse ways. Its role in seasonal cooking and festivals, particularly in springtime celebrations, further underscores its importance as a cherished ingredient. Understanding these ancient beginnings provides a foundation for appreciating rhubarb's rich history and its enduring place in contemporary cooking and cuisine.

The Journey to Europe: Trade and Cultivation

The journey of rhubarb to Europe is a tale steeped in trade and cultivation that significantly shaped its culinary and medicinal uses. Originally native to the regions of Siberia and China, rhubarb was first cultivated for its roots, which were prized for their medicinal properties. As trade routes expanded, particularly along the Silk Road, this once obscure plant found its way into the hands of European traders and botanists. By the 14th century, rhubarb began to emerge in Europe, captivating the interest of herbalists and chefs alike. The initial fascination with its medicinal qualities laid the groundwork for its eventual culinary applications, thereby intertwining health and gastronomy in a rich historical tapestry.

Once established in Europe, rhubarb's cultivation practices evolved dramatically. Early European gardeners recognized the benefits of growing rhubarb not just for its roots but also for its tart stalks. The climate of regions such as the United Kingdom, with its cool, moist conditions, proved to be ideal for rhubarb cultivation. Gardeners began to experiment with different varieties, leading to the development of the famous forced rhubarb, which is grown in darkened sheds to produce tender, sweet stalks. This method not only enhanced the flavor but also allowed for an earlier harvest, making it a seasonal delicacy celebrated in various culinary traditions.

The role of rhubarb in traditional medicine during this period cannot be overstated. Various cultures across Europe utilized rhubarb for its health benefits, from aiding digestion to acting as a detoxifying agent. Folklore surrounding rhubarb often highlighted these medicinal uses, with tales of its ability to cure ailments passed down through generations. This dual identity as both a food and a remedy cemented rhubarb's place in the hearts of many, creating a strong cultural significance that would influence regional recipes and practices.

As rhubarb became more popular in European kitchens, its versatility in cooking was further explored. Different regions developed unique rhubarb varieties, each with distinct flavors and textures that inspired a range of recipes. In England, for instance, rhubarb was often combined with sugar to create delicious crumbles and pies, while in France, it was frequently featured in tarts and compotes. The evolution of rhubarb recipes across cultures reflected not only local tastes but also the changing perceptions of rhubarb, from a medicinal herb to a culinary staple. This evolution showcases how one ingredient can adapt and thrive in various gastronomic landscapes.

Today, rhubarb continues to play a significant role in modern gastronomy, where chefs embrace its tartness and unique flavor profile. Seasonal cooking and local festivals often celebrate rhubarb, highlighting its importance in the agricultural calendar. As we delve into the intricacies of rhubarb pairings, preservation techniques, and its impact on contemporary dishes, we uncover a rich history that connects generations of cooks, healers, and food enthusiasts. The journey to Europe not only brought rhubarb to our tables but also expanded our culinary horizons, making it a beloved ingredient in kitchens worldwide.

Rhubarb in America: Adoption and Adaptation

Rhubarb, a plant with origins tracing back to ancient China, found its way to America in the 17th century, where it was initially cultivated for medicinal purposes. The adoption of rhubarb in the New World was influenced by both European settlers and Indigenous peoples, each contributing to its early use in various contexts. As settlers recognized rhubarb's versatility, it transitioned from a curiosity in early colonial gardens to an ingredient explored in numerous culinary applications. This subchapter delves into the journey of rhubarb in America, highlighting how it was embraced, adapted, and eventually celebrated in American cuisine.

The unique climate of North America has played a significant role in the adaptation of rhubarb varieties. While the plant flourished in the cooler regions of the Northeast, it found a home in other areas, such as the Midwest, where farmers cultivated it extensively. The differences in soil types and climate conditions led to the development of distinct regional varieties. For instance, the tartness of the popular 'Victoria' rhubarb differs from the sweetness of the 'Crimson Cherry' variety. These regional adaptations not only influenced flavor profiles but also shaped local culinary traditions, with each area incorporating rhubarb into its seasonal dishes and celebrations.

Rhubarb's culinary evolution in America is a testament to its adaptability. Early American recipes often mirrored European traditions, featuring rhubarb in pies, jams, and sauces. However, as American cooks began to experiment with local ingredients, rhubarb recipes transformed, incorporating flavors such as strawberries, ginger, and citrus. This melding of influences led to the creation of unique dishes, such as the beloved strawberry rhubarb pie, which has become a staple in many households. The evolution of rhubarb recipes showcases a broader trend in American cooking, where immigrant influences and regional ingredients converge to create a distinctive culinary identity.

In addition to its culinary uses, rhubarb has a storied place in traditional medicine and folklore. Many early settlers relied on rhubarb for its purported health benefits, using it as a remedy for digestive issues and other ailments. This medicinal heritage has been interwoven into the narratives surrounding rhubarb, contributing to its status as a nostalgic ingredient in American kitchens. Recipes often invoke memories of family gatherings and seasonal rituals, reinforcing the cultural significance of rhubarb as more than just a food item but a means of connection to history and heritage.

Today, rhubarb continues to inspire chefs and home cooks alike, adapting to modern gastronomy while maintaining its historical roots. As culinary trends shift towards sustainability and seasonal cooking, rhubarb is celebrated not just for its unique flavor but also for its role in promoting local agriculture. Preservation techniques such as canning and freezing allow enthusiasts to enjoy rhubarb year round, ensuring that this resilient plant remains a cherished part of American culinary culture. The journey of rhubarb in America is ongoing, reflecting the dynamic interplay of tradition and innovation that characterizes the nation's evolving food landscape.

Chapter 2:

Historical Cultivation Practices of Rhubarb

Traditional Growing Techniques

Traditional growing techniques for rhubarb have been passed down through generations, reflecting a rich history intertwined with culinary practices and medicinal uses. Originally cultivated in Asia, rhubarb made its way to Europe in the 17th century, where it quickly gained popularity not just for its unique tart flavor, but also for its therapeutic properties. Understanding these traditional cultivation methods provides insight into how this resilient plant has thrived in various climates and soils, making it a staple in many gardens.

One of the most important aspects of traditional rhubarb cultivation is the selection of the right location. Rhubarb prefers well drained, fertile soil and thrives in areas with full sun to partial shade. Gardeners have historically chosen sites that provide shelter from strong winds and extreme temperatures, ensuring that the plants could produce robust stalks. The soil is often enriched with organic matter, such as compost or well rotted manure, which not only fosters healthy growth but also enhances the flavor of the rhubarb. This symbiotic relationship between the plant and its environment is crucial for achieving the best yield.

Planting rhubarb is typically done in early spring or fall, with the crowns essentially the root system of the plant being planted about three feet apart to allow for their expansive growth. Traditional methods emphasize the importance of patience, as rhubarb requires a few seasons to establish itself before it can be harvested. Careful attention is given to the watering schedule, especially during dry spells, as consistent moisture is key to producing tender, flavorful stalks. Additionally, many growers utilize mulch to retain soil moisture and suppress weeds, which can otherwise compete for nutrients.

Harvesting techniques also play a vital role in the traditional cultivation of rhubarb. It is essential to harvest the stalks by pulling them gently from the base rather than cutting, as this method encourages further growth. Traditionally, only the outermost stalks are harvested, allowing the inner ones to continue maturing. This practice not only ensures a continuous supply throughout the growing season but also maintains the health of the plant for future harvests. Growers often wait until the plant has reached maturity, typically around the third year, to maximize both quantity and quality.

In addition to its culinary uses, rhubarb has long been embraced for its medicinal properties, which have been celebrated in folklore and traditional medicine. Knowledge of these practices has been passed down through families and communities, enhancing the cultural significance of rhubarb. Whether it's a comforting rhubarb pie at a seasonal festival or a homemade tincture for digestive ailments, the traditional growing techniques of rhubarb serve as a testament to the enduring relationship between people and this remarkable plant. Understanding these methods not only enriches our appreciation of rhubarb but also inspires us to explore its many uses in contemporary recipes and culinary adventures.

The Role of Rhubarb in Early Gardens

The role of rhubarb in early gardens is a fascinating chapter in the culinary history of this unique plant. Known for its tart flavor and vibrant stalks, rhubarb has been cultivated for centuries, finding its place not only in kitchens but also in gardens across various cultures. Early gardeners recognized the plant's versatility and nutritional benefits, leading to its inclusion in home gardens as a staple for both culinary and medicinal purposes. This subchapter explores how rhubarb became an essential crop, the practices surrounding its cultivation, and its significance in early culinary traditions.

In many historical gardens, rhubarb was valued for its hardiness and ability to thrive in diverse climates. Its early introduction to Europe from Asia during the 14th century marked the beginning of its journey into European cuisine. Gardeners appreciated its resilience, particularly in cooler climates where other crops struggled. The rhubarb plant not only provided a source of food but also added vibrant colors to the garden landscape, making it an esthetically pleasing choice. As a perennial plant, it symbolized continuity and sustenance, thriving year after year with minimal care once established.

Traditional cultivation practices of rhubarb varied by region, reflecting local agricultural knowledge and conditions. In England, for example, rhubarb was often grown in rich, moist soil and received careful attention to its growing environment. Gardeners would plant it in early spring, allowing the stalks to mature for harvesting in late spring and early summer. This seasonal cycle made rhubarb a focal point in early summer cooking, leading to a plethora of recipes that highlighted its unique flavor profile. Across different cultures, the cultivation of rhubarb was often accompanied by specific rituals and methods, ensuring that the plant flourished and produced its renowned stalks.

Beyond its culinary uses, rhubarb also held a place in traditional medicine, where its leaves were sometimes utilized for their purported health benefits. Folklore surrounding rhubarb often emphasized its role in healing and wellness, with various cultures attributing different medicinal properties to the plant. Early herbalists recognized the value of rhubarb in treating ailments, incorporating it into remedies for digestive issues and other health concerns. The integration of rhubarb into both gardens and medicine illustrates its multifaceted role in early societies, serving as a bridge between nourishment and healing.

As rhubarb spread across continents, it adapted to different climates and regional culinary traditions, leading to the emergence of unique varieties. Each region developed its own methods of cultivation and uses for rhubarb, resulting in a rich tapestry of flavors and preparations. In the United States, for instance, varieties like the popular 'Victoria' and 'Crimson Red' were embraced for their sweetness and vibrant color, often finding their way into pies and preserves. The evolution of rhubarb recipes highlights how this humble plant has transcended its garden origins to become a cherished ingredient in diverse cuisines, celebrated for its ability to pair harmoniously with various flavors.

The importance of rhubarb in early gardens underscores its role as a resilient and versatile plant that has captivated gardeners and cooks alike. From its cultivation practices to its culinary and medicinal uses, rhubarb has woven itself into the fabric of food history. As we explore the depths of rhubarb's significance, we uncover not only its journey through time but also its enduring appeal in modern gastronomy, where it continues to inspire chefs and home cooks in creative culinary expressions.

Cultivation Challenges Through the Ages

Cultivation challenges have always played a significant role in shaping the history and culinary uses of rhubarb. As one of the earliest cultivated plants, rhubarb has encountered various obstacles throughout different periods, influencing its growth, popularity, and culinary application. The journey of rhubarb from its wild origins to a staple in gardens and kitchens across the globe illustrates not only its resilience but also the adaptive strategies employed by gardeners and farmers. The challenges faced in rhubarb cultivation have often mirrored the agricultural practices and environmental conditions of the time, revealing much about human ingenuity in the face of adversity.

In ancient times, rhubarb was primarily valued for its medicinal properties rather than its culinary potential. The harsh climates of its native habitats, particularly in regions like Siberia and Mongolia, posed significant challenges for early cultivators. These conditions required innovative methods of cultivation, such as selecting hardy varieties capable of withstanding cold temperatures and poor soil conditions. Historically, gardeners learned to manipulate soil quality and microclimates to encourage growth, which laid the groundwork for the eventual culinary exploration of the plant. The transition from a primarily medicinal herb to a culinary ingredient came as cultivation techniques improved and societal attitudes towards rhubarb shifted.

The Industrial Revolution marked a significant turning point in rhubarb cultivation, as advancements in agricultural technology and transportation allowed for broader distribution and cultivation practices. However, this era also introduced new challenges, such as soil degradation and the advent of pests and diseases that could devastate crops. Farmers began to adopt more systemic approaches to cultivation, including crop rotation and the use of fertilizers, to maintain healthy rhubarb crops. These practices not only enhanced yields but also provided a deeper understanding of the plant's requirements, setting the stage for the diverse range of rhubarb recipes that would emerge in the culinary world.

In the 20th century, the introduction of hybrid varieties and increased focus on sustainable agriculture transformed rhubarb cultivation once again. While these innovations helped to address some of the previous challenges, they also led to new concerns regarding biodiversity and the preservation of traditional rhubarb strains. Gardeners began to appreciate regional varieties, recognizing their unique flavors and uses in local cuisines. This revival of interest in heirloom and regional rhubarb varieties not only enriched culinary practices but also fostered a deeper connection to the land and its history, emphasizing the importance of preserving agricultural heritage in modern times.

Today, as climate change continues to impact agricultural practices, rhubarb cultivators face a new set of challenges. Fluctuating temperatures and unpredictable weather patterns threaten the delicate balance required for successful rhubarb growth. Nevertheless, the lessons learned from centuries of cultivation challenges inspire resilience and adaptability among contemporary growers. Their efforts to implement sustainable practices, experiment with new varieties, and adapt to changing climates ensure that rhubarb remains a cherished ingredient in kitchens, celebrated for its unique tartness and versatility. As we delve deeper into the culinary history of rhubarb, it becomes clear that understanding these cultivation challenges enriches our appreciation for this remarkable plant and the many delicious recipes it inspires.

Chapter 3:

Rhubarb in Traditional Medicine: Folklore and Facts

Medicinal Uses in Ancient Cultures

Rhubarb's storied past extends far beyond its culinary applications, as ancient cultures recognized the plant for its medicinal properties long before it became a staple ingredient in pies and jams. The roots of rhubarb, specifically, were prized for their potential health benefits, leading to their use in traditional medicine across various civilizations. Ancient Chinese herbalists documented the use of rhubarb as early as 2700 BCE, employing it primarily as a purgative and to treat gastrointestinal issues. This early recognition of rhubarb's medicinal potential laid the groundwork for its enduring reputation in herbal medicine.

In addition to its use in China, rhubarb made its mark in the medical practices of the Middle Ages. European herbalists began to explore the plant's properties, incorporating it into treatments for a variety of ailments. Rhubarb's high content of anthraquinones, compounds known for their laxative effects, positioned it as a favored remedy for constipation. Medieval texts often recommended rhubarb root in tinctures and decoctions, highlighting its role not only as a digestive aid but also as a treatment for fevers and inflammation. This versatility underscored rhubarb's significance within the broader context of herbal medicine during this era. The spread of rhubarb throughout Europe brought about regional adaptations in its use. In the 17th century, when rhubarb was introduced to England from Asia, it quickly gained popularity not only in kitchens but also in apothecaries. Herbalists began to combine rhubarb with other botanicals to enhance its medicinal efficacy. For instance, it was often paired with ginger or cinnamon in concoctions aimed at improving digestion and overall health. This blending of flavors and therapeutic properties showcased the evolving understanding of rhubarb as both a culinary and medicinal ingredient.

Indigenous cultures also recognized the value of rhubarb in their traditional healing practices. In North America, Native American tribes utilized the plant for its medicinal attributes, employing it to treat various ailments such as fevers, wounds, and digestive issues. The root was commonly dried and ground into a powder to be used in herbal remedies. Such practices reflect a deep rooted understanding of natural resources and their potential to foster health, illustrating the plant's significance beyond mere sustenance.

As we delve into the rich history of rhubarb, it becomes evident that its medicinal uses in ancient cultures played a pivotal role in shaping perceptions of the plant. The transition from a revered medicinal herb to a beloved culinary ingredient highlights the multifaceted nature of rhubarb throughout history. By exploring these ancient applications, modern enthusiasts can appreciate not only the unique flavors of rhubarb but also its legacy as a natural remedy, enriching our understanding of this remarkable plant as we incorporate it into our own kitchens today.

Folklore and Myths Surrounding Rhubarb

Folklore and myths surrounding rhubarb are as rich and varied as the plant itself, weaving a complex narrative that spans cultures and centuries. Rhubarb, often viewed as a humble garden vegetable, has been imbued with mystical qualities in many traditions. In some European folklore, it was believed that rhubarb could ward off evil spirits and protect homes from misfortune. This protective quality was so esteemed that rhubarb was sometimes planted near doorways or windows. Such beliefs illustrate how this vibrant plant transcended its culinary uses to become a symbol of safety and security in the domestic sphere.

In addition to its protective attributes, rhubarb has also been the subject of numerous myths regarding its medicinal properties. Traditionally, rhubarb has been used in herbal medicine, particularly in Chinese culture, where it is revered as a remedy for various ailments, including digestive issues and inflammation. The ancient texts of Chinese herbalists often extolled the virtues of rhubarb root, believed to possess powerful purifying qualities. However, it is crucial to distinguish between the culinary stalk and the medicinal root; while the stalk is safe to eat, the root can be toxic in large quantities, highlighting the importance of understanding and respecting the plant's dual nature.

Regional variations of rhubarb folklore further illustrate its significance in different cultures. In North America, rhubarb has become associated with springtime celebrations, often heralded as one of the first crops to emerge from the thawing ground. This seasonal awakening has inspired local festivals, where communities gather to celebrate the arrival of this tart vegetable with pie baking contests and rhubarb themed events. These traditions not only emphasize the culinary potential of rhubarb but also strengthen community bonds and celebrate the agricultural heritage of the region.

Rhubarb's presence in literature and art has also played a role in shaping its folklore. Poets and writers throughout history have used rhubarb as a symbol of nostalgia and the changing seasons. In various literary works, its vibrant color and unique flavor are often described as representative of childhood and the simple pleasures of life. Artists have depicted rhubarb in still life compositions, showcasing its aesthetic appeal and inviting viewers to appreciate its beauty beyond the kitchen. Such representations have contributed to the plant's mythos, elevating it from a mere garden vegetable to a cultural icon.

As we explore the rich tapestry of folklore and myths surrounding rhubarb, it becomes clear that this remarkable plant serves as a bridge between the past and present. Its stories, steeped in tradition and cultural significance, enrich our understanding of rhubarb not just as an ingredient, but as a symbol of resilience and community. This exploration invites food enthusiasts to engage with rhubarb in new ways, encouraging them to honor its historical roots while experimenting with modern culinary applications. In the following recipes and discussions, we will continue to unravel the many layers of this intriguing plant, celebrating both its culinary versatility and the folklore that has shaped its identity over the centuries.

Modern Scientific Insights

Modern scientific insights into rhubarb have significantly enhanced our understanding of this versatile plant, which has been cherished for centuries not only for its culinary potential but also for its medicinal properties. Recent research has shed light on the nutritional benefits of rhubarb, revealing that it is rich in vitamins C and K, as well as fiber, making it a valuable addition to a healthy diet. Studies indicate that the antioxidants found in rhubarb may contribute to reducing inflammation and oxidative stress in the body, suggesting that incorporating this tart vegetable into meals can have positive health implications.

In addition to its nutritional value, modern agricultural practices have transformed the way rhubarb is cultivated. Advances in horticultural science have led to the development of hybrid varieties that boast improved yields and disease resistance. These innovations have made it easier for farmers to grow rhubarb in diverse climates, thereby expanding its availability in markets year round. Understanding the specific growth requirements and optimal conditions for rhubarb cultivation, such as soil pH and moisture levels, has allowed growers to produce high quality rhubarb that meets the demands of both home cooks and professional chefs.

Moreover, contemporary studies have revisited rhubarb's role in traditional medicine, examining the folklore that has surrounded this plant for generations. While historical uses of rhubarb often included treatments for digestive issues and other ailments, modern scientific scrutiny has validated some of these claims while debunking others. This ongoing exploration serves to bridge the gap between ancient practices and contemporary dietary guidelines, suggesting that while rhubarb can be beneficial, it should be consumed with an understanding of its properties and potential risks, particularly when it comes to its oxalic acid content.

The evolution of rhubarb recipes in various cultures also reflects changing culinary trends and preferences. Today, chefs are embracing rhubarb not just as a dessert ingredient, but as a versatile component in savory dishes. The modern culinary landscape has witnessed a resurgence in the use of rhubarb in sauces, salads, and even cocktails, demonstrating its adaptability and ability to enhance a wide range of flavors. This shift aligns with the growing interest in seasonal cooking, where fresh, local ingredients are prioritized, and rhubarb, often one of the first plants to emerge in spring, fits this ethos perfectly.

Finally, understanding the impact of climate on rhubarb growth is crucial in our current era of climate change. Research has been conducted to analyze how shifting weather patterns affect rhubarb's growth cycles, yield, and flavor profile. Such insights not only inform farmers on best practices for cultivation but also guide chefs and home cooks in selecting the best varieties for their dishes. By staying attuned to these scientific advancements, we can better appreciate rhubarb's place in our kitchens and on our plates, ensuring that this historical vegetable remains a beloved ingredient for generations to come.

Chapter 4:

Regional Rhubarb Varieties and Their Unique Uses

Common Varieties and Their Characteristics

Rhubarb, often celebrated for its tart flavor and vibrant color, comes in several varieties, each with unique characteristics that cater to different culinary applications. The most common types include the Standard Garden Rhubarb, the Victoria, the Champagne, and the Green Rhubarb. Each variety not only differs in taste and texture but also in its suitability for various recipes, ranging from pies and jams to savory dishes. Understanding these distinctions can enhance your cooking experience and help, you choose the right rhubarb for your culinary creations.

Standard Garden Rhubarb is the most widely recognized variety, distinguishable by its thick, red stalks and large leaves. This type has a robust tartness that makes it ideal for desserts, especially pies and crumbles. Its high acidity balances well with sweet ingredients, making it a favorite in many traditional recipes. When harvested early in the season, the stalks are tender and less fibrous, providing a delightful mouthfeel in baked goods.

This rhubarb variety is often the go to for home gardeners and culinary enthusiasts alike due to its versatility and availability. The Victoria variety, known for its bright red stalks and tender texture, is another popular choice. It is particularly prized for its sweetness compared to other types, which allows it to shine in both sweet and savory applications. The Victoria rhubarb is often used in jams, preserves, and desserts, but it can also be incorporated into salads or paired with meats for a zesty contrast. Its slightly milder flavor profile makes it a favorite among those who may find standard rhubarb too tart, thus broadening its appeal in various dishes.

Champagne rhubarb, with its pale pink to light green stalks, is celebrated for its delicate flavor and tenderness. This variety is often regarded as the best choice for making compotes and syrups due to its subtle sweetness and appealing texture when cooked. The Champagne variety is less acidic, which allows it to be used in a wide range of culinary contexts, including as a topping for yogurt or ice cream, or even in cocktails. Its elegant appearance and gentle flavor make it a sophisticated addition to any culinary repertoire.

Lastly, Green Rhubarb, often overlooked, offers a different taste experience. While it may not have the vivid color of its red counterparts, this variety brings a unique earthy note to dishes. Its stalks are thicker and can be slightly more fibrous, requiring longer cooking times to tenderize. Green Rhubarb is excellent in savory applications, such as stews or braises, where its flavor can complement other ingredients without overwhelming them. By exploring these common varieties and their characteristics, cooks can elevate their dishes and embrace the full culinary potential of rhubarb.

Regional Specialties: From Yorkshire to the Americas

Regional specialties often reflect the unique climate, culture, and culinary traditions of a specific area, and rhubarb is no exception. From the rolling hills of Yorkshire to the vibrant markets of the Americas, this versatile plant has found its place in a variety of regional dishes. In Yorkshire, rhubarb is celebrated as a local treasure, particularly the famed forced rhubarb, which is grown in dark sheds to produce tender, sweet stalks. The region's long standing fascination with rhubarb has led to numerous recipes that showcase its tartness, such as the classic Yorkshire rhubarb crumble, where the fruit's acidity is beautifully balanced with a rich, buttery crumble topping.

Across the Atlantic, the Americas have embraced rhubarb in equally creative ways. In the Midwest, where the plant thrives in fertile soils, rhubarb pie has become a seasonal staple, often enjoyed during spring and early summer. This dessert embodies the spirit of local cooking, utilizing simple ingredients to highlight the tartness of rhubarb. American cooks have adapted traditional recipes, incorporating spices like ginger and nutmeg, which complement the rhubarb's natural flavors while adding a touch of warmth. This evolution of rhubarb recipes in the Americas showcases the adaptability of this ingredient and the creative spirit of regional cooking.

In addition to its culinary uses, rhubarb has played a role in traditional medicine and folklore in various cultures. In Yorkshire, folklore often depicts rhubarb as a remedy for ailments, with tales passed down through generations highlighting its purported health benefits. Similarly, indigenous communities across North America have utilized rhubarb for its medicinal properties, using it in teas and tinctures. As we explore the intersection of rhubarb and traditional medicine, it becomes clear that this plant is not only valued for its culinary applications but also for its historical significance in various healing practices.

The diversity of regional rhubarb varieties further enriches its culinary landscape. Different climates and soil conditions yield distinct flavors and textures, from the tartness of the common garden rhubarb to the sweet nuances of specialized varieties like the Victoria and the Crimson. Each type offers unique opportunities for experimentation in the kitchen, inspiring chefs and home cooks alike to develop recipes that reflect their local heritage. As we delve into the unique uses of these varieties, we discover how they can be paired with local ingredients, creating dishes that celebrate both the rhubarb and the region.

As we explore the culinary journey of rhubarb from Yorkshire to the Americas, it becomes evident that this humble plant has woven itself into the fabric of regional cuisine. Its adaptability and vibrant flavors have inspired countless recipes across cultures, making it a beloved ingredient for seasonal cooking and festive celebrations. The evolution of rhubarb in different culinary contexts not only showcases its versatility but also highlights the importance of preserving traditional practices and celebrating local flavors. As we continue to uncover rhubarb's rich history and diverse applications, we invite you to embrace this remarkable ingredient in your own kitchen, creating dishes that honor both its legacy and your local culinary traditions.

Unique Uses in Local Cuisines

Subchapter: Unique Uses in Local Cuisines

Rhubarb, with its tangy flavor and vibrant hue, has carved out a significant place in various local cuisines around the globe. Each region has adapted this versatile plant, creating unique dishes that reflect local tastes and culinary traditions. From the traditional rhubarb pie of North America to the savory rhubarb stews found in parts of the Middle East, the creativity surrounding rhubarb's use is limited only by the imagination of the cook. This subchapter delves into the diverse applications of rhubarb in regional dishes, celebrating its versatility and historical significance in culinary practices.

In England, rhubarb has long been a staple, particularly in Yorkshire, where it is often referred to as "Yorkshire rhubarb."

This region's cold climate is ideal for rhubarb cultivation, leading to an abundance of this ingredient. Yorkshire rhubarb is traditionally used in desserts, with the classic rhubarb crumble or fool showcasing its sweet and tart balance. These dishes not only highlight the fruit's natural flavors but also embody the traditional British ethos of enjoying seasonal produce. The emphasis on local sourcing and seasonal cooking has kept these recipes alive through generations, making rhubarb a beloved ingredient in English households.

Moving across the Channel to Scandinavia, rhubarb finds its way into both sweet and savory dishes. In Sweden, for instance, rhubarb is often incorporated into jams and syrups, which serve as accompaniments to various pastries and breakfast dishes. Additionally, savory rhubarb sauces are used to complement Ash, providing a refreshing contrast to the rich flavors of the sea. The Scandinavian approach to rhubarb showcases its adaptability, demonstrating how it can bridge the gap between sweet and savory profiles, much like other regional ingredients that play dual roles in cuisine.

In the United States, rhubarb is particularly celebrated in the Midwest, where it has become emblematic of springtime and home cooked comfort food. Midwestern kitchens frequently utilize rhubarb in pies, crisps, and jams, often pairing it with strawberries to create a harmonious blend of flavors. These dishes not only satisfy the palate but also evoke nostalgia, connecting individuals to family gatherings and seasonal traditions. Furthermore, the popularity of rhubarb in local farmer's markets highlights the region's commitment to supporting sustainable agriculture and showcasing local produce.

Lastly, in regions like Asia, rhubarb takes on a different role, often featured in medicinal dishes rather than sweet treats. In Traditional Chinese Medicine, for example, rhubarb (known as "dahuang") has been used for centuries for its purported health benefits, including its ability to support digestive health. The incorporation of rhubarb in herbal remedies and soups illustrates its significance beyond culinary applications, revealing a rich tapestry of cultural beliefs and practices surrounding this unique ingredient. As we explore these varied uses of rhubarb across local cuisines, it becomes clear that this humble plant is much more than a simple ingredient; it is a reflection of cultural identity and historical practices that continue to evolve.

Chapter 5:

Rhubarb in Literature and Art Throughout History

Rhubarb as a Symbol in Literature

Rhubarb, with its vibrant stalks and tart flavor, has made its mark not only in kitchens but also in the pages of literature. As a symbol, rhubarb often represents resilience, regeneration, and the complexities of human experience. Writers have harnessed its unique characteristics to evoke themes of nostalgia, hardship, and the bittersweet nature of life. Understanding these literary allusions can deepen our appreciation for rhubarb, elevating it from mere culinary ingredient to a profound cultural symbol that resonates through various narratives.

In classical literature, rhubarb appears as a metaphor for the passage of time and the cycles of nature. Its seasonal growth and harvest reflect the rhythms of human life, making it an apt representation of renewal and growth. Authors have often used rhubarb to illustrate the tension between the harshness of winter and the promise of spring, paralleling characters' journeys as they navigate their own struggles and transformations. This connection to the natural world reinforces rhubarb's role as a symbol of hope and resilience, serving as a reminder that new beginnings often emerge from difficult circumstances.

Rhubarb's symbolism extends into the realm of domesticity and comfort. In many literary works, it is associated with home cooked meals and the warmth of family gatherings. The preparation of rhubarb dishes can evoke memories of childhood, representing a return to simpler times and the bonds forged through shared culinary experiences. This association with nostalgia highlights the emotional connections we have with food and the stories that unfold around the dinner table, showcasing rhubarb not just as an ingredient but as a vessel for cherished memories and traditions.

Moreover, rhubarb has been used in literature to explore themes of transience and loss. The fleeting nature of its season mirrors the ephemeral qualities of life, prompting reflections on mortality and the inevitability of change. Authors have employed rhubarb in this context to illustrate characters grappling with their own impermanence, reminding readers that even the most vibrant experiences can be bittersweet. This duality of rhubarb its ability to evoke joy while simultaneously hinting at sorrow imbues literary works with a rich complexity, prompting deeper contemplation of the human condition.

As we delve into the culinary history and recipes featuring rhubarb, it becomes clear that its literary significance enhances our understanding of this remarkable plant. By recognizing rhubarb as a symbol in literature, we can appreciate its multifaceted role in storytelling and its connection to the broader tapestry of human experiences. Whether in the form of a tart pie or a refreshing compote, rhubarb continues to inspire both writers and cooks alike, serving as a delicious reminder of the narratives woven into our food and culture.

Artistic Representations of Rhubarb

Artistic representations of rhubarb reveal much about its cultural significance and the ways it has inspired creativity throughout history. From classical paintings to contemporary illustrations, rhubarb has been depicted not merely as a humble vegetable but as a symbol of abundance and the changing seasons. Artists have often captured its vibrant stalks and lush leaves, celebrating its unique form and color, which evoke a sense of freshness and vitality. This artistic exploration provides insights into how rhubarb has been perceived and valued across different eras and societies.

In historical contexts, rhubarb was often associated with the bounty of the earth and the pleasures of the harvest. Many still life paintings from the 17th century feature rhubarb prominently alongside other seasonal produce, illustrating its importance in the culinary landscape of the time. These artworks highlight the connections between food, nature, and art, fostering an appreciation for the aesthetics of ingredients that grace our tables. Notably, artists like the Dutch masters employed meticulous attention to detail in their depictions, symbolizing not only the beauty of the ingredients but also the care and effort involved in cultivation and preparation.

Rhubarb's role extends beyond the canvas; it has also found a place in literature and poetry, often serving as a metaphor for resilience and renewal. Writers have drawn upon the imagery of rhubarb to evoke themes of growth and transformation, paralleling the plant's seasonal cycles with human experiences. This literary exploration offers a deeper understanding of how food can resonate with emotional and cultural narratives, enriching the culinary experience. Rhubarb becomes more than just an ingredient; it is a vessel for storytelling, connecting generations through shared memories of gardens, kitchens, and meals.

In contemporary art, rhubarb continues to inspire, showing its versatility not only as a subject but also as a medium. Modern artists experiment with the plant's vivid colors and textures, creating works that challenge traditional perceptions of food and art. This fusion of culinary and artistic practices reflects a broader trend in which chefs and artists collaborate, blurring the boundaries between gastronomy and visual expression. Such initiatives encourage audiences to view rhubarb through multiple lenses, appreciating its role in both the culinary arts and the broader cultural dialogue.

Ultimately, artistic representations of rhubarb are a testament to its enduring appeal and multifaceted nature. Whether through paintings, poetry, or contemporary artwork, rhubarb serves as a reminder of the deep connections between food, culture, and creativity. As we explore its history and culinary applications, we also celebrate the artistic expressions that elevate this remarkable plant, inviting us to appreciate not only its flavor but also its beauty and significance in our lives.

Rhubarb in Popular Culture

Rhubarb's presence in popular culture extends beyond the kitchen, weaving itself into literature, art, and even music. This vibrant plant has captured the imagination of many creators throughout history. In literature, rhubarb often symbolizes the passage of seasons and the joys of spring, reflecting its growth and harvest cycles. For instance, in various works of English literature, rhubarb appears as a metaphor for renewal and abundance, serving as a reminder of nature's gifts and the pleasures of culinary creativity. Authors have used the plant to illustrate the connection between food, memory, and the experiences of domestic life, highlighting its role in the home kitchen.

In the visual arts, rhubarb has made its mark through paintings and illustrations that celebrate its unique aesthetic. Artists often depict rhubarb's striking colors deep reds and greens drawing attention to its textural contrasts and structural forms. These representations not only elevate the humble vegetable to the status of an art subject but also reflect cultural attitudes toward food and nature. The rhubarb plant's bold appearance makes it an attractive subject for still life compositions, often symbolizing abundance and the beauty of the natural world. Through such artistic expressions, rhubarb is transformed from mere ingredient to an emblem of seasonal change and culinary tradition.

The culinary world has also embraced rhubarb, leading to its inclusion in various popular media, including cookbooks, television shows, and social media platforms. Chefs and food enthusiasts alike have utilized rhubarb to create innovative recipes that highlight its tartness and versatility. From traditional pies to modern savory dishes, rhubarb has found its place in contemporary gastronomy. Food bloggers and influencers have played a significant role in reviving interest in rhubarb, sharing eye catching images and creative pairings that inspire home cooks to experiment. This resurgence in popularity is a testament to rhubarb's adaptability and enduring appeal across different culinary landscapes.

Rhubarb has also made its way into music and folklore, often celebrating the joys of rural life and seasonal harvests. Folklore surrounding rhubarb varies by region, with tales often highlighting its medicinal properties and role in local traditions. Songs and stories that mention rhubarb evoke nostalgia and a connection to the land, reflecting the plant's historical significance in various communities. Festivals centered around rhubarb, such as rhubarb pie contests and harvest celebrations, bring people together, fostering a sense of community and shared culinary heritage. These events not only promote the enjoyment of rhubarb but also emphasize its role in cultural identity and local pride.

The intersection of rhubarb with popular culture demonstrates its multifaceted significance, affirming its status as a beloved ingredient and symbol. As we explore rhubarb's culinary history and its evolving use in recipes, it becomes clear that this remarkable plant has transcended its role as a simple garden vegetable. Instead, it has become a cultural touchstone that connects us to our past, inspires creativity in the kitchen, and encourages communal celebrations of food and culture. In this way, rhubarb continues to thrive in both culinary and cultural realms, inviting all those who appreciate food to partake in its rich narrative.

Chapter 6:

The Evolution of Rhubarb Recipes in Different Cultures Historical Recipes and Their Transformations

Historical recipes often carry with them the weight of cultural narratives and culinary evolution, and rhubarb is no exception. This vibrant plant, with its tart flavor and vivid stalks, has found its way into kitchens around the world, transforming alongside the societies that cultivate it. From its early use in ancient medicine to its role in contemporary gastronomy, rhubarb recipes have undergone significant changes, reflecting shifts in taste, availability, and culinary techniques. By exploring these transformations, we can gain insight into how rhubarb has become a beloved ingredient in both traditional and modern kitchens.

In ancient times, rhubarb was primarily valued for its medicinal properties rather than its culinary potential. Early recipes often featured rhubarb in tinctures and tonics, as its astringent qualities were believed to aid digestion and detoxification. As the plant gradually gained popularity as a food source, early recipes began to emerge, showcasing rhubarb's tartness in pies and preserves. These original preparations were simple, relying on minimal ingredients to highlight the plant's natural flavors. Over the centuries, as trade routes expanded and culinary techniques evolved, rhubarb began to be incorporated into a wider array of dishes, paving the way for the diverse recipes we enjoy today.

The transformation of rhubarb recipes can also be seen through the lens of regional practices and cultural influences. In the United Kingdom, for instance, rhubarb became synonymous with springtime, leading to the creation of traditional dishes like rhubarb crumble and fool. Meanwhile, in North America, early settlers adapted European recipes, resulting in unique creations like rhubarb pie, which became a staple in many households. Each region's approach to rhubarb reflects local tastes, available ingredients, and cultural significance, demonstrating how this versatile plant has been embraced and reinterpreted across diverse culinary landscapes.

As we move into the modern era, rhubarb has found its place in contemporary gastronomy, inspiring chefs to experiment with innovative pairings and techniques. The rise of farm to table dining has reinvigorated interest in seasonal ingredients, and rhubarb's short growing season makes it a prized component in many dishes. Chefs are now exploring its potential beyond desserts, incorporating it into savory dishes, sauces, and even beverages. This evolution not only showcases rhubarb's versatility but also highlights a broader trend in the culinary world where traditional ingredients are reimagined for modern palates.

Preservation techniques have also played a significant role in the ongoing transformation of rhubarb recipes. Historically, canning and freezing methods allowed cooks to enjoy rhubarb even after its peak season, leading to an increase in its use throughout the year. Today, these techniques continue to be relevant, as home cooks seek ways to extend the life of seasonal produce. The ability to preserve rhubarb has opened up new avenues for creativity, allowing for the development of recipes that celebrate the plant's flavors in unexpected ways. By examining the historical recipes and their transformations, we can appreciate the journey of rhubarb from its humble origins to its esteemed status in both traditional and modern culinary practices.

Cultural Variations in Rhubarb Dishes

Cultural variations in rhubarb dishes reflect the diverse culinary traditions and regional practices that have evolved over centuries. This unique vegetable, often classified as a fruit in the culinary world, has found its way into numerous cuisines, each adapting it to local tastes and customs. From the tartness of rhubarb pie in North America to the sweet and savory chutneys of Indian cuisine, rhubarb showcases its versatility as an ingredient that can enhance both sweet and savory dishes. Understanding these variations not only enriches our appreciation for rhubarb but also opens up a world of culinary exploration.

In North America, rhubarb is often celebrated in desserts, with the classic rhubarb pie being a star attraction during spring and summer. This dish typically highlights a blend of sugar and spices to balance the vegetable's tartness, reflecting the region's preference for sweet desserts. Recipes often call for a buttery crust that complements the tangy filling, creating a delightful contrast. Beyond pies, rhubarb is also used in crumbles, jams, and sauces, showcasing its adaptability to various sweet preparations. These dishes often carry nostalgic significance for many, evoking memories of family gatherings and seasonal harvests.

In contrast, European cuisines have a different approach to rhubarb. In the United Kingdom, for instance, rhubarb is a staple in springtime desserts, but it is also commonly used in savory applications. Rhubarb compote can be served alongside roasted meats, providing a refreshing acidity that cuts through rich flavors. The English tradition of pairing rhubarb with ginger in both sweet and savory dishes exemplifies how regional tastes shape the culinary use of this vegetable. Additionally, traditional recipes often reflect the local agricultural practices, incorporating other seasonal ingredients to create a harmonious dish that celebrates the harvest.

Asian cuisines, particularly in India, utilize rhubarb in a unique way, transforming it into spicy chutneys and pickles. The tartness of rhubarb pairs beautifully with the bold spices typical of Indian cooking, such as mustard seeds, turmeric, and chili. These chutneys serve as a condiment that enhances the accompanying dishes, showcasing how rhubarb can easily adapt to different flavor profiles. This cultural variation illustrates the global appreciation of rhubarb as an ingredient that transcends its original culinary context, allowing it to flourish in diverse settings.

Exploring rhubarb in various cultural contexts highlights the ingredient's ability to inspire creativity among chefs and home cooks alike. Each region's historical cultivation practices, local flavors, and culinary traditions shape how rhubarb is utilized, resulting in a rich tapestry of dishes that celebrate its unique characteristics. As we delve into the recipes and stories from different cultures, we not only discover new ways to enjoy rhubarb but also gain insight into the shared human experience of cooking and sharing food. Embracing these cultural variations can inspire innovative approaches in our own kitchens, inviting us to experiment with rhubarb in ways that honor both tradition and personal taste.

Modern Interpretations and Innovations

Modern interpretations and innovations in rhubarb cuisine reflect the fruit's rich history while embracing contemporary culinary trends. Chefs and home cooks alike are reimagining classic rhubarb recipes, employing techniques that elevate this tart vegetable into the spotlight of modern gastronomy. As a versatile ingredient, rhubarb finds its way into both sweet and savory dishes, demonstrating its ability to adapt to various culinary styles and preferences. This subchapter delves into the innovative approaches to rhubarb, highlighting how it has been transformed in kitchens across the globe.

One significant innovation is the incorporation of rhubarb into savory dishes, a departure from its traditional role in desserts. Chefs are experimenting with rhubarb chutneys, sauces, and even salads, where its tartness acts as a counterbalance to richer flavors. For instance, a rhubarb and ginger relish can complement grilled meats, while a rhubarb infused vinaigrette adds a refreshing twist to leafy greens. These modern interpretations not only showcase rhubarb's versatility but also reflect a growing trend of incorporating unexpected ingredients into savory culinary applications.

In addition to savory innovations, the use of advanced techniques such as sous vide and molecular gastronomy is making waves in the culinary world. These methods allow for precise control over the cooking process, enhancing the natural flavors and textures of rhubarb. Sous vide rhubarb, for example, can be cooked to perfect tenderness without losing its vibrant color, resulting in a visually stunning dish. Meanwhile, molecular gastronomy techniques, such as creating rhubarb foam or gel, provide an exciting dining experience that invites diners to engage with rhubarb in new and unexpected ways.

The rise of plant based diets has also influenced rhubarb's role in modern cuisine. As more individuals seek to incorporate fruits and vegetables into their meals, rhubarb has emerged as a popular choice due to its unique flavor profile and nutritional benefits. Innovative recipes featuring rhubarb in vegan desserts, such as rhubarb coconut sorbet or rhubarb almond bars, highlight its adaptability and ability to shine without relying on animal products. This shift towards plant based cooking not only promotes sustainability but also encourages creativity in utilizing rhubarb as a key ingredient.

Finally, the trend of seasonal cooking and farm to table dining has further solidified rhubarb's place in modern culinary practices. Chefs are increasingly focusing on sourcing local, seasonal ingredients, and rhubarb, with its spring harvest, fits perfectly into this ethos. Festivals celebrating rhubarb have sprung up in various regions, showcasing local varieties and unique applications. At these events, home cooks and professional chefs alike share recipes that highlight the distinct flavors of rhubarb, fostering a sense of community and appreciation for this historically rich ingredient. Through these modern interpretations and innovations, rhubarb continues to evolve, proving that it is much more than a relic of the past.

Chapter 7:

Rhubarb Preservation Techniques: Canning and Freezing

Methods of Preservation

Preserving rhubarb is an essential aspect for those who wish to enjoy its tart flavor long after the growing season has ended. The methods of preservation not only extend the shelf life of this vibrant vegetable but also allow home cooks to explore its versatility throughout the year. Canning and freezing are two popular techniques that effectively capture the essence of rhubarb, ensuring that its unique taste and nutritional benefits remain intact. Understanding these methods can elevate your culinary repertoire and enable you to incorporate rhubarb into various dishes, regardless of the season.

Canning rhubarb involves cooking it with sugar and sometimes other ingredients to create a delicious preserve or compote. This method is particularly favored for its ability to enhance the rhubarb's natural flavors while adding a touch of sweetness. The traditional canning process requires sterilizing jars and processing them in a water bath or pressure canner to ensure safety. When done correctly, canned rhubarb can last for up to a year, making it a wonderful addition to desserts like pies, tarts, and even as a topping for yogurt or pancakes. The canning process not only preserves the fruit but also allows for experimentation with spices and flavorings, adding depth to traditional recipes.

Freezing is another effective method for preserving rhubarb, particularly if you want to retain its texture and freshness. This technique involves cleaning, chopping, and blanching the rhubarb briefly before placing it in airtight containers or freezer bags. Properly frozen rhubarb can maintain its quality for up to a year, making it a convenient option for those who want to enjoy its vibrant flavor during the off season. When you're ready to use it, frozen rhubarb can be incorporated directly into recipes without the need for thawing, making it an ideal ingredient for crumbles, smoothies, and sauces.

Both canning and freezing allow for the preservation of rhubarb while maintaining its nutritional value, which is particularly important for health conscious individuals. Rhubarb is low in calories and high in vitamins K and C, as well as dietary fiber. By employing these preservation methods, you can ensure that you are not only enjoying the delightful taste of rhubarb but also reaping its health benefits throughout the year. Additionally, these techniques encourage sustainability by reducing food waste, as excess rhubarb can be easily stored and enjoyed later.

In conclusion, mastering the methods of preservation for rhubarb is a rewarding endeavor that opens the door to a myriad of culinary possibilities. Whether you choose to can or freeze your rhubarb, each method offers unique advantages that can enhance your cooking experience. As you explore the world of rhubarb, you'll find that these preservation techniques not only extend its shelf life but also inspire creativity in the kitchen, allowing you to celebrate this remarkable ingredient in various dishes and celebrations year round.

Best Practices for Canning Rhubarb

Canning rhubarb is an excellent way to preserve its tangy flavor and vibrant color, allowing you to enjoy this unique vegetable long after its growing season has ended. Best practices for canning rhubarb not only ensure food safety but also maintain the quality and taste of the final product. Before embarking on your canning adventure, it is essential to familiarize yourself with the necessary equipment and ingredients to achieve optimal results. Start with fresh, young rhubarb stalks, as they are more tender and flavorful. Look for stalks that are firm and brightly colored, avoiding any that are wilted or discolored.

Preparation is critical in the canning process. Begin by thoroughly washing the rhubarb to remove any dirt and pesticides, then trim the ends and cut the stalks into uniform pieces, generally about 1 inch in length. This ensures even cooking and promotes better packing in jars. Depending on your recipe, you may choose to blanch the rhubarb briefly in boiling water to preserve its color and texture, although this step can be skipped if you prefer a firmer consistency. Once prepared, the rhubarb can be combined with sugar, spices, or other fruits to enhance its natural tartness, creating a delicious compote or filling.

When it comes to the actual canning process, it is crucial to follow tested recipes and guidelines to ensure safety. Use sterilized glass jars and lids, which can be achieved by boiling them in water for ten minutes. Fill the jars with prepared rhubarb, leaving appropriate headspace as indicated in your recipe. This space allows for the expansion of food as it heats during the canning process. After sealing the jars with the lids, process them in a boiling water bath for the recommended time, which varies depending on the size of the jars and the specific recipe used.

Cooling and storing the canned rhubarb correctly is just as

important as the preparation and processing stages. Once the jars have been removed from the boiling water, allow them to cool at room temperature. You should hear a "pop" sound as the lids seal, indicating a proper vacuum seal has formed. After they are fully cooled, check the seals by pressing down in the center of each lid; if it doesn't spring back, it is sealed correctly. Store the sealed jars in a cool, dark place. Properly canned rhubarb can last for up to a year, retaining its flavor and texture for use in pies, sauces, and other dishes.

In conclusion, canning rhubarb is a straightforward and rewarding endeavor for anyone who appreciates this versatile ingredient. By adhering to best practices in preparation, processing, and storage, you can create delicious canned rhubarb that captures the essence of this unique vegetable. The benefits of canning extend beyond mere preservation; they allow you to explore a variety of culinary applications that showcase rhubarb's tangy flavor. Whether enjoyed in a homemade pie or as a topping for yogurt, canned rhubarb is sure to be a delightful addition to your pantry.

Freezing Rhubarb: Tips and Tricks

Freezing rhubarb is an excellent way to preserve its tart flavor and vibrant color, allowing you to enjoy this unique ingredient long after its seasonal harvest. Whether you've just returned from a fruitful trip to the local farm or have a bountiful garden, freezing rhubarb can extend its shelf life and provide you with a versatile ingredient for a variety of dishes. This subchapter offers essential tips and tricks to ensure your frozen rhubarb retains its flavor and texture for future culinary adventures.

Before freezing, it's crucial to prepare your rhubarb correctly. Start by selecting fresh, healthy stalks that are Arm and vibrant in color, as these will yield the best results. Wash the stalks thoroughly to remove any dirt or debris, and trim off any leaves, which are toxic.

Next, cut the rhubarb into uniform pieces typically around 1 inch segments so that they freeze evenly. If you plan to use the rhubarb in recipes that require cooking, such as pies or jams, blanching the pieces for one to two minutes in boiling water can help preserve their texture and color.

Once prepared, it's time to freeze the rhubarb. Lay the cut pieces in a single layer on a baking sheet and place them in the freezer for a few hours until they are firm. This process, known as flash freezing, prevents the pieces from clumping together, allowing for easier portioning later on. After the rhubarb is frozen solid, transfer the pieces into airtight freezer bags or containers, removing as much air as possible to prevent freezer burn. Label the bags with the date, as frozen rhubarb is best used within 8 to 12 months for optimal quality.

When it comes to using frozen rhubarb in your recipes, there's no need to thaw it beforehand if you're incorporating it into baked goods. Frozen rhubarb can be added directly to pies, crumbles, and sauces, although you may need to adjust the cooking time slightly. If you prefer to use it in smoothies or savory dishes, thawing the rhubarb in the refrigerator or using a microwave can help you achieve the desired texture. Keep in mind that frozen rhubarb may release more moisture than fresh, so adjusting the liquid in your recipes may be necessary to maintain balance.

In addition to its practical benefits, freezing rhubarb allows you to explore its culinary versatility year round. From traditional desserts like rhubarb pie to creative uses in savory dishes and sauces, the preserved tartness of frozen rhubarb can elevate a variety of recipes. By mastering the art of freezing rhubarb, you can savor the taste of this historical ingredient throughout the seasons, celebrating its rich heritage while experimenting with modern gastronomy.

Chapter 8:

Rhubarb as an Ingredient in Modern Gastronomy

Rhubarb in Contemporary Cuisine

Rhubarb has long been celebrated for its tart flavor and vibrant color, but its role in contemporary cuisine has evolved dramatically over the past few decades. Chefs and home cooks alike have embraced this unique vegetable, transforming it into a versatile ingredient that enhances a wide array of dishes. From savory to sweet, rhubarb's distinct tanginess can elevate everything from sauces and marinades to desserts and cocktails. This subchapter will explore how rhubarb has found its place in modern culinary practices, showcasing its adaptability and appeal.

One notable trend in contemporary cuisine is the incorporation of rhubarb in savory dishes. No longer relegated solely to desserts, chefs are experimenting with rhubarb in salads, chutneys, and even as a component in meat dishes. The tartness of rhubarb can cut through rich flavors, providing a refreshing contrast that enhances the overall palate. For example, rhubarb can be pickled and served alongside grilled meats, or it can be blended into a sauce that complements roasted vegetables. This versatility allows cooks to leverage rhubarb's bold flavor profile in unexpected ways, demonstrating its potential beyond traditional uses.

Modern gastronomy also sees rhubarb paired with an eclectic

range of ingredients, reflecting the global influences that characterize contemporary cooking. Chefs are increasingly mixing rhubarb with spices, herbs, and other fruits to create innovative flavor combinations. For instance, rhubarb and ginger work beautifully together, as the warmth of ginger balances the acidity of rhubarb. Similarly, pairing rhubarb with strawberries in a tart or jam is a classic approach that remains popular, but contemporary chefs are also exploring combinations with unexpected ingredients like chili, basil, or even chocolate, showcasing the ingredient's versatility and encouraging culinary creativity.

Preservation techniques have also evolved, allowing rhubarb to be enjoyed year round. While canning and freezing remain popular methods, modern techniques such as sous vide and dehydrating have opened new avenues for preserving rhubarb's flavors and textures. This not only extends the ingredient's shelf life but also allows for its use in out of season dishes. Seasonal cooking remains a hallmark of contemporary cuisine, and with the ability to preserve rhubarb effectively, chefs can incorporate its vibrant taste into menus even when fresh rhubarb is unavailable.

As culinary trends continue to shift towards sustainability and local sourcing, rhubarb is emerging as a star ingredient in farm to table movements. Many chefs are now sourcing rhubarb from local farms, celebrating its unique regional varieties and the story behind each harvest. Seasonal festivals dedicated to rhubarb are also gaining popularity, where communities come together to showcase the vegetable in all its forms. By highlighting rhubarb's role in contemporary cuisine, we not only honor its rich history but also pave the way for future culinary explorations that embrace this remarkable ingredient.

Innovative Chefs and Their Rhubarb Creations

Innovative chefs are redefining the culinary landscape by

embracing rhubarb, a versatile ingredient often overshadowed by more popular fruits. These culinary artists are not only experimenting with traditional recipes but are also pushing the boundaries of what rhubarb can achieve in modern gastronomy. Their creations highlight the unique tartness and vibrant color of rhubarb, transforming it into dishes that surprise and delight diners. From savory applications to avant garde desserts, these innovative chefs are breathing new life into this historic ingredient, showcasing its potential and versatility.

One notable trend among chefs is the incorporation of rhubarb into savory dishes. By pairing rhubarb with proteins such as pork or chicken, chefs create a harmonious balance of flavors that elevates the dining experience. For instance, rhubarb can be used in salsas, glazes, or reductions, providing a refreshing acidity that cuts through richness and enhances the overall dish. This innovative approach not only showcases rhubarb's flavor profile but also reimagines traditional culinary practices, encouraging home cooks to experiment with unconventional pairings.

Desserts, of course, remain a cherished domain for rhubarb. Chefs are reinterpreting classic rhubarb dishes, such as pies and crumbles, by infusing contemporary techniques and global flavors. For example, rhubarb can be paired with spices like cardamom or ginger, or transformed into sorbets and mousses that reflect seasonal preferences. These modern takes not only honor the ingredient's rich heritage but also inspire a new generation of food enthusiasts to appreciate rhubarb in all its forms. By utilizing molecular gastronomy techniques, some chefs even create rhubarb foams or gels that add an exciting visual and textural element to their desserts.

Regional varieties of rhubarb also play a crucial role in these innovative culinary endeavors. Chefs are increasingly sourcing specific types of rhubarb that thrive in their local climates, which adds a unique twist to their dishes. For instance, the sweeter varieties found in certain regions lend themselves to desserts, while the more tart varieties are perfect for savory applications. This not only promotes regional agriculture but also encourages a deeper connection between chefs and their local food systems, allowing them to showcase the diversity of rhubarb and its unique characteristics.

As the culinary world continues to evolve, the role of rhubarb in seasonal cooking and festivals is gaining renewed attention. Chefs are tapping into the nostalgia associated with rhubarb, often using it as a centerpiece in spring menus to celebrate the arrival of warmer weather. By incorporating rhubarb into special events and culinary festivals, these chefs highlight its cultural significance and encourage diners to explore the history and folklore surrounding this remarkable plant. Through their innovative rhubarb creations, chefs are not just preparing food; they are telling a story that connects past and present, tradition and innovation, all through the vibrant lens of rhubarb.

Rhubarb in Fine Dining

Rhubarb has long transcended its humble beginnings as a garden staple to find its place in the realm of fine dining. Chefs and culinary artists have embraced this unique vegetable, known for its tart flavor and vibrant color, transforming it into exquisite dishes that delight the senses. In fine dining, rhubarb is celebrated not just for its taste but also for its versatility, allowing it to be featured in appetizers, mains, and desserts. Its ability to pair harmoniously with a variety of ingredients opens up a world of culinary possibilities, making it a favored choice among innovative chefs looking to elevate their menus.

The evolution of rhubarb in fine dining can be traced back to its historical significance and culinary heritage. Once primarily used in traditional medicine and simple home cooking, rhubarb has been reimagined in gourmet kitchens. Modern chefs often incorporate rhubarb into their dishes to reflect seasonal changes, highlighting its availability in spring and early summer. This adherence to seasonality not only pays homage to the ingredient's roots but also aligns with contemporary diners' increasing preferences for fresh, locally sourced produce.

Pairings play a crucial role in rhubarb's appeal in fine dining. Chefs expertly combine rhubarb with complementary flavors such as strawberries, ginger, and citrus to create balanced dishes that tantalize the palate. Its acidity can cut through rich flavors, making it an ideal component in sauces and glazes for meats, while also serving as a bright contrast in desserts. The ability to balance sweetness and tartness allows rhubarb to shine in both savory and sweet applications, showcasing its adaptability and inviting creativity in the kitchen.

Rhubarb's presence in fine dining is not just limited to traditional recipes; it has also inspired avant garde culinary techniques. Molecular gastronomy, for instance, has seen the use of rhubarb in foams, gels, and other textural innovations that challenge the conventional perceptions of this ingredient. Chefs are experimenting with pickling, fermenting, and smoking rhubarb, pushing the boundaries of flavor and presentation. These modern interpretations not only highlight the ingredient's potential but also engage diners in a sensory experience that celebrates the artistry of cooking.

As fine dining continues to evolve, the role of rhubarb remains firmly rooted in its rich history while adapting to contemporary tastes and techniques. Its journey from a traditional garden plant to a sophisticated culinary element reflects broader trends in the food industry that emphasize sustainability, creativity, and seasonal cooking. By incorporating rhubarb into fine dining menus, chefs honor its legacy and invite diners to explore its diverse applications, ensuring that this remarkable ingredient remains a vibrant part of the culinary landscape for years to come.

Chapter 9:

The Role of Rhubarb in Seasonal Cooking and Festivals

Rhubarb Harvesting Seasons

Rhubarb harvesting seasons are a fascinating aspect of this unique plant that connects culinary enthusiasts with the rhythms of nature. Generally, rhubarb is harvested in the spring and early summer months, a time when the stalks are at their most tender and flavorful. In temperate regions, the primary harvesting period typically begins in April and can extend through June, depending on local climate conditions. The timing of the harvest is critical; harvesting too early may yield stalks that are too small and tart, while waiting too long can lead to tougher textures and a more pronounced bitterness.

The specific harvesting times can vary by region due to climate differences. For example, in cooler northern climates, rhubarb may take longer to mature, with the peak harvest occurring in late spring. Conversely, in warmer southern regions, rhubarb can be ready for harvest as early as March. Understanding these regional nuances not only enhances the appreciation of rhubarb's culinary uses but also allows cooks to source the freshest ingredients available, aligning their recipes with seasonal produce for optimal flavor and quality.

Historical cultivation practices have also influenced the timing and methods of harvesting rhubarb. Traditionally, farmers would harvest rhubarb by hand, using a gentle twisting motion to detach the stalks from the plant. This method minimizes damage to the root system and promotes healthy regrowth for subsequent harvests. In many cultures, the first harvest of the season is celebrated, often coinciding with local festivals that honor spring and the bounty it brings. These practices highlight the deep cultural connections that have developed around rhubarb cultivation and harvesting, making it a significant part of agricultural heritage.

Rhubarb's role in traditional medicine further emphasizes its seasonal importance. Folklore often associates the spring harvest with rejuvenation and health, as the plant is believed to have various medicinal properties. Historically, rhubarb was used as a natural remedy for ailments ranging from digestive issues to skin conditions. The timing of the harvest aligns with the belief that spring foods can cleanse and revitalize the body after the long winter months, making rhubarb not only a culinary delight but also a symbol of seasonal renewal.

In modern gastronomy, the understanding of rhubarb harvesting seasons informs a variety of culinary practices. Chefs and home cooks alike are encouraged to embrace the fleeting nature of rhubarb's peak season by incorporating it into seasonal menus and recipes. Whether it's a tangy rhubarb compote, a vibrant pie, or a refreshing rhubarb cocktail, the unique tartness and vivid color of fresh rhubarb can elevate dishes and provide a connection to the earth's cycles. By honoring the harvesting seasons, culinary enthusiasts can create memorable experiences that celebrate both the rich history of rhubarb and its versatile role in contemporary cooking.

Festivals Celebrating Rhubarb

Festivals celebrating rhubarb have become a delightful way to honor this unique vegetable, transforming it from a culinary staple into a center of community celebration. These events not only showcase the versatility of rhubarb in various dishes but also highlight its rich history and cultural significance. From the charming small town gatherings to larger regional festivals, each event serves as a platform for locals and visitors alike to come together in appreciation of this tart ingredient. Festival goers can expect a vibrant atmosphere filled with food tastings, cooking demonstrations, and the sharing of rhubarb lore, all while enjoying the company of fellow food enthusiasts.

One of the most notable rhubarb festivals is the annual Rhubarb Festival held in the quaint town of Berrien Springs, Michigan. This festival has grown over the years, attracting thousands of visitors eager to savor rhubarb infused delicacies. Attendees can indulge in a variety of culinary creations, including rhubarb pies, jams, and even beverages, all prepared by local chefs and home cooks. The festival also features contests, such as "Best Rhubarb Dessert," where participants showcase their creativity and skill, further fostering a sense of community spirit around this beloved plant.

In addition to culinary offerings, these festivals often delve into the historical cultivation practices of rhubarb, educating attendees about its origins and the traditional methods of growing this hardy vegetable. Workshops and presentations led by local farmers and historians provide insight into how rhubarb has been cultivated over centuries, transforming from a medicinal herb to a cherished ingredient in modern cooking. Such educational components not only enrich the experience for visitors but also ensure that the knowledge surrounding rhubarb cultivation and its uses is passed down through generations.

Furthermore, many rhubarb festivals celebrate the diversity of regional rhubarb varieties and their unique uses. Different areas have developed their own strains of rhubarb, each with distinct flavors and characteristics. For instance, the pink hued varieties popular in the Midwest are often sweeter, making them ideal for desserts, while the more robust green varieties found in other regions lend themselves well to savory applications. By sampling dishes that highlight these regional differences, festival attendees can gain a broader understanding of rhubarb's culinary potential and how it has adapted to different climates and cooking traditions.

Ultimately, festivals celebrating rhubarb serve as a microcosm of food culture, emphasizing the importance of seasonal ingredients and the joy of community gatherings centered around shared culinary experiences. They offer a unique opportunity for people to not only taste and enjoy rhubarb in its many forms but also to connect with the history and traditions that accompany this remarkable vegetable. As these festivals continue to grow in popularity, they play a vital role in keeping the spirit of rhubarb alive, ensuring that its legacy as a versatile ingredient remains vibrant and relevant in the culinary world.

Seasonal Recipes Featuring Rhubarb

Rhubarb, with its vibrant hue and tart flavor, is a quintessential ingredient that marks the arrival of spring in many kitchens. As the first produce to emerge from the thawing earth, it has long been celebrated in seasonal recipes that highlight its unique characteristics. From pies to preserves, rhubarb's versatility allows it to shine in a variety of culinary applications. This subchapter will explore several delightful seasonal recipes that not only honor rhubarb's rich history but also incorporate modern cooking techniques, making it accessible to anyone who enjoys food and wants to experiment in the kitchen.

One classic recipe that showcases the bright acidity of rhubarb is the traditional rhubarb pie. This dish has deep historical roots, tracing back to early American settlers who cultivated rhubarb in their gardens. The pie typically combines rhubarb with sugar to balance its tartness, often enhanced with spices like cinnamon or nutmeg. For a modern twist, consider adding a crumb topping made with oats and brown sugar, which adds texture and depth. Serving this pie warm with a scoop of vanilla ice cream transforms a simple dessert into a seasonal celebration, evoking nostalgia for summer picnics and family gatherings.

Another way to embrace the seasonal bounty of rhubarb is through its incorporation into savory dishes. A rhubarb chutney, for instance, pairs perfectly with grilled meats or as a condiment for sandwiches. This recipe combines diced rhubarb with onions, ginger, and a touch of vinegar, simmered until the ingredients meld into a tangy, flavorful sauce. Such dishes reflect historical cultivation practices where rhubarb was not just relegated to sweet treats but also utilized for its bold flavor in savory contexts. This versatility highlights the ingredient's role in regional cuisines and encourages cooks to think beyond the traditional sweet applications.

For those interested in preserving the taste of rhubarb beyond its brief growing season, canning and freezing techniques are invaluable. A simple rhubarb compote can be made by cooking down rhubarb with sugar and a splash of lemon juice, which can then be stored in sterilized jars. This compote can be used throughout the year, dolloped on yogurt, pancakes, or incorporated into baked goods. The preservation of rhubarb not only allows for year round enjoyment but also connects to historical practices where seasonal ingredients were preserved to sustain households through the winter months.

Finally, as we explore the role of rhubarb in seasonal cooking, it is essential to consider its pairings with other ingredients. Rhubarb's tartness complements flavors like strawberries, ginger, and citrus, making it a dynamic player in fruit salads, smoothies, and sauces. A refreshing rhubarb strawberry salad, for example, combines the two fruits with a zesty dressing, creating a vibrant centerpiece for spring gatherings. Highlighting these complementary flavors not only enriches dishes but also emphasizes the importance of seasonal ingredients in creating balanced and harmonious meals. Through these recipes, home cooks can celebrate rhubarb's legacy and versatility, forging a connection between the past and present in their culinary adventures.

Chapter 10:

Rhubarb Pairings: Exploring Complementary Flavors

Sweet Pairings: Sugars and Spices

Rhubarb, with its vibrant crimson stalks and tart flavor, has long been celebrated in culinary traditions for its unique versatility. One of the most delightful aspects of working with this perennial plant is the way it pairs beautifully with various sugars and spices, enhancing its natural tang and creating layers of flavor that excite the palate. Understanding these sweet pairings not only enriches rhubarb dishes but also deepens our appreciation for its historical significance and culinary evolution across cultures.

Historically, rhubarb was often combined with different sweeteners to balance its inherent tartness. Traditional recipes frequently featured sugar, honey, or molasses, which were used not only to sweeten but also to preserve the fruit's vibrant color and texture. In medieval Europe, for instance, rhubarb was prized for its medicinal qualities and was often combined with honey in herbal remedies. This sweetening not only made the medicine more palatable but also showcased the plant's dual role as both a culinary delight and a healthful ingredient.

When it comes to spices, rhubarb's bright acidity offers a perfect canvas for experimentation. Cinnamon, ginger, and nutmeg have long been favored companions, adding warmth and depth to rhubarb dishes. The combination of rhubarb and ginger, for example, is a classic pairing in many cultures, from the pies of North America to the chutneys of India. These spices not only enhance the flavor profile but also evoke a sense of nostalgia, reminding us of the comfort of home cooked meals and shared traditions.

Regional variations also play a significant role in the development of rhubarb recipes that utilize sugars and spices. In the American South, for example, rhubarb is often sweetened with brown sugar and spiced with nutmeg or allspice, resulting in a rich, caramelized flavor that complements the tartness of the stalks. Conversely, in Scandinavian countries, rhubarb is typically paired with cardamom, reflecting the local palate and culinary customs. Exploring these regional nuances not only broadens our culinary horizons but also highlights the adaptability of rhubarb across different cultures and cuisines.

In modern gastronomy, chefs are increasingly creative with rhubarb, incorporating it into unexpected pairings that challenge traditional notions. Today you might find rhubarb paired with exotic spices like star anise or even infused with floral notes such as lavender. These innovative combinations not only celebrate rhubarb's unique flavor but also invite food lovers to experiment in their kitchens. As we explore the sweet pairings of sugars and spices with rhubarb, we open the door to a world of culinary possibilities, honoring the rich history of this remarkable plant while inspiring new generations of home cooks to embrace its vibrant essence.

Savory Combinations: Meats and Vegetables

Savory Combinations: Meats and Vegetables explores the

intriguing ways in which rhubarb can enhance and elevate meat and vegetable dishes. Historically, rhubarb has been cherished not only for its tartness but also for its ability to balance rich flavors. In various cultures, cooks have utilized this unique ingredient to create delightful contrasts that invigorate traditional recipes. By pairing rhubarb with meats and vegetables, one can discover a culinary synergy that is both delicious and rooted in history.

Rhubarb's natural acidity makes it an excellent companion for fatty meats, such as pork or duck. The tartness cuts through the richness, providing a refreshing counterbalance. For instance, rhubarb and pork belly have been a classic combination in many cultures, with the rhubarb often prepared as a sauce or compote. This pairing not only enhances the flavor of the dish but also pays homage to historical practices where seasonal produce was used to preserve and complement meats. As cooks sought to make the most of their harvests, rhubarb became a staple in these savory combinations.

Vegetables, too, benefit from the addition of rhubarb. When paired with hearty greens or root vegetables, rhubarb can add a surprising twist. The tangy notes of rhubarb can brighten dishes like roasted beets or sautéed kale, lifting the earthy flavors and creating a more vibrant plate. This approach reflects the historical cultivation practices of rhubarb, which often emphasized the importance of utilizing seasonal vegetables alongside available meats. Such combinations reflect a farm to table philosophy that has stood the test of time and continues to inspire modern gastronomy.

In terms of regional rhubarb varieties, different types can lend unique flavors to savory dishes. For example, the tartness of an early season rhubarb can differ significantly from that of a later harvest. Understanding these nuances allows cooks to select the ideal rhubarb for their recipes, enhancing the overall dish. This knowledge is further enriched by exploring folk traditions that have long celebrated specific varieties of rhubarb in local cuisines, showcasing how geography and culture influence culinary practices.

Ultimately, the exploration of savory combinations involving rhubarb is a journey through history and flavor. As we delve into these pairings, we not only uncover the evolution of rhubarb recipes across cultures but also recognize the significance of using what is locally available. Whether one is looking to experiment with new flavors or honor traditional methods, incorporating rhubarb with meats and vegetables offers a delicious way to celebrate this versatile ingredient. In doing so, we connect with a rich culinary heritage that continues to inspire and delight food lovers today.

Beverage Pairings with Rhubarb

Rhubarb's unique tartness and vibrant color make it a delightful ingredient not just in food, but also in beverages. When considering pairing drinks with rhubarb, it's essential to think about how its acidity can balance sweetness, enhance flavors, and create refreshing combinations. From cocktails to teas, the versatility of rhubarb can elevate any drink, making it a worthy companion in your culinary explorations. This section discusses several beverage options that harmonize beautifully with rhubarb, enhancing its natural characteristics while providing a refreshing experience.

One of the most popular ways to incorporate rhubarb into beverages is through cocktails. Rhubarb syrup, made by simmering rhubarb with sugar and water, can serve as a base for various drinks. When paired with gin, the herbal notes complement the rhubarb's tartness, creating a refreshing and bright cocktail. Additionally, combining rhubarb syrup with sparkling wine or prosecco results in a delightful spritz, perfect for summer gatherings. These combinations not only highlight the rhubarb's flavor but also showcase its ability to blend seamlessly with other spirits, making it a favorite among mixologists.

Non alcoholic beverages also benefit from the addition of rhubarb. A rhubarb lemonade, for instance, captures the essence of summer with its tangy and sweet profile. The rhubarb's acidity enhances the brightness of the lemon, while its natural sweetness balances the drink perfectly. Herbal teas are another avenue to explore; steeping rhubarb with mint or chamomile can yield a soothing and fragrant infusion. This versatility in non alcoholic drinks allows those who prefer to abstain from alcohol to enjoy the refreshing qualities of rhubarb in various forms.

For those interested in more traditional beverages, rhubarb can be a surprising yet delightful addition to smoothies. Blending rhubarb with seasonal fruits like strawberries or apples yields a nutrient rich, vibrant drink that captures the essence of spring. The tartness of the rhubarb cuts through the sweetness of the fruits, creating a balanced flavor profile that is both refreshing and satisfying. Experimenting with yogurt or almond milk can further enhance the creamy texture of the smoothie, making it a perfect breakfast or snack option.

Lastly, rhubarb can find its way into warm beverages as well. A hot rhubarb cider, made by simmering rhubarb with apple cider and spices like cinnamon and cloves, offers a cozy and inviting drink, perfect for cooler months. This warm concoction not only celebrates rhubarb's versatility but also emphasizes its ability to provide comfort and warmth. By exploring these beverage pairings, one can appreciate rhubarb not only as a culinary ingredient but also as a key player in the world of drinks, celebrating its rich history and diverse applications across cultures.

Chapter 11:

The Impact of Climate on Rhubarb Growth and Culinary Uses

Climate Requirements for Optimal Growth

Climate requirements play a crucial role in the successful cultivation of rhubarb, a perennial vegetable renowned for its tart flavor and vibrant stalks. Understanding the environmental conditions that favor its growth can help gardeners and chefs alike appreciate not only the plant's culinary potential but also its historical significance. Rhubarb thrives best in temperate climates, where it can benefit from a distinct seasonal change. This ensures a pronounced dormancy period during the colder months, which is essential for the plant's health and vigor come spring.

Temperature is one of the most critical factors influencing rhubarb growth. Ideal daytime temperatures range from 60 to 75 degrees Fahrenheit, while nighttime temperatures should not drop below 40 degrees. These conditions promote robust leaf development and the production of juicy, flavorful stalks. In regions where summers soar above 80 degrees, rhubarb may struggle; prolonged heat can cause the plant to bolt, leading to flowering and a decrease in the quality of the edible stalks. Thus, gardeners should consider their local climate when selecting rhubarb varieties, ensuring they choose types that will perform well in their specific conditions.

Moisture levels also significantly impact rhubarb cultivation. Rhubarb requires consistently moist soil to thrive, as its large leaves need ample hydration. However, it's essential to maintain well draining soil to prevent waterlogging, which can lead to root rot. Regular watering, especially during dry spells, is necessary to keep the soil evenly moist. Mulching can help retain soil moisture while also suppressing weeds that compete for water and nutrients. For those in regions with less predictable rainfall, implementing a drip irrigation system can provide a steady supply of moisture without oversaturating the roots.

Sunlight is another fundamental aspect of rhubarb cultivation. The plant flourishes best in full sun, which typically means at least six hours of direct sunlight per day. In areas with intense heat, some afternoon shade can help protect rhubarb from scorching, allowing it to thrive without compromising flavor. When planting rhubarb, it's wise to consider its placement in the garden situating it where it can receive optimal sunlight while being sheltered from harsh winds can significantly influence its growth and yield.

Finally, understanding the seasonal nuances of your climate can enhance your rhubarb harvest. In many regions, rhubarb is one of the first crops to emerge in the spring, signaling the arrival of the growing season. Harvesting should typically occur from late spring to early summer, as this is when the stalks are at their peak flavor and texture. By aligning planting and harvesting practices with local climate patterns, both home gardeners and culinary enthusiasts can maximize their rhubarb production and enjoy this unique ingredient in a variety of dishes. With the right climate conditions, rhubarb not only flourishes but also enriches the culinary landscape with its vibrant presence.

Regional Climate Variations and Their Effects

Regional climate variations significantly influence the growth, flavor, and culinary applications of rhubarb, a versatile and historically rich plant.

Different climates from temperate to subtropical affect not only the rate of rhubarb's growth but also the characteristics of the stalks that are harvested. In cooler regions, such as parts of the United Kingdom and the northern United States, rhubarb tends to develop a more tart flavor profile, which makes it an ideal candidate for pies, crumbles, and other desserts that benefit from a sharp contrast to sweetness. Conversely, in warmer climates, rhubarb can have a milder and sweeter taste, opening up a range of culinary possibilities including salads and savory dishes.

Soil composition and moisture levels, both of which are heavily influenced by climate, further contribute to the diversity of rhubarb varieties. For example, in regions with rich, loamy soils and consistent rainfall, like the Pacific Northwest, rhubarb grows plentifully and achieves impressive sizes. These conditions create stalks that are not only larger but also juicier, thus enhancing their use in sauces and jams. Meanwhile, in drier climates where water is scarce, rhubarb may be smaller and more fibrous, which may lead to its use as a flavoring component rather than the star of the dish.

Culinary traditions surrounding rhubarb also adapt to regional climate variations. In colder areas, where rhubarb thrives in the spring and early summer, it becomes a key ingredient in seasonal cooking, often celebrated in local festivals and food events. Recipes from these regions often highlight rhubarb's tartness through traditional desserts and preserve making. In contrast, cultures in warmer regions may incorporate rhubarb into lighter dishes, such as refreshing salads or unique sauces that complement grilled meats. These regional differences showcase how climate shapes not only the growth of rhubarb but also the culinary creativity surrounding it.

The impact of climate on rhubarb extends beyond flavor and texture; it also influences harvest times and preservation techniques. In cooler climates, rhubarb is typically harvested in late spring to early summer, leading to preservation methods like canning and freezing to extend its usability throughout the year. This practice is often reflected in historic recipes that were designed to make the most of the short rhubarb growing season. In contrast, in warmer climates, where rhubarb can be grown year round, fresh preparations take precedence, allowing for more immediate culinary experimentation and less reliance on preservation.

Understanding the regional climate variations not only enriches our appreciation of rhubarb's versatility but also highlights the importance of local practices in shaping culinary traditions. As we delve into the myriad ways rhubarb has been incorporated into recipes across cultures and regions, it becomes clear that these differences are a celebration of nature's bounty and human ingenuity. Whether you're drawn to the tangy burst of a classic rhubarb pie or the innovative uses of rhubarb in modern gastronomy, recognizing how climate defines these experiences can deepen our connection to this remarkable plant and its rich culinary history.

Adapting Rhubarb Cultivation to Climate Change

Adapting rhubarb cultivation to the challenges posed by climate change is becoming increasingly vital as shifts in weather patterns affect growing conditions worldwide. Historically, rhubarb has thrived in cooler climates, but as average temperatures rise and precipitation patterns fluctuate, growers must innovate to ensure successful harvests. This subchapter explores practical strategies for adjusting cultivation practices to maintain rhubarb's role in our culinary landscape while considering the environmental changes that threaten its traditional growing conditions.

One of the key adaptations involves selecting appropriate rhubarb varieties that are more resilient to heat and drought. Recent breeding efforts have focused on developing cultivars that can withstand warmer temperatures while maintaining the tart flavor and vibrant color that make rhubarb a favorite in both sweet and savory dishes. Gardeners can also experiment with regional varieties, which may possess unique adaptations to local climates. By diversifying the types of rhubarb planted, growers can enhance their chances of success and contribute to the preservation of genetic diversity within the species.

Soil management practices will also play a critical role in adapting rhubarb cultivation to a changing climate. With the increasing frequency of extreme weather events, such as heavy rainfall and prolonged dry spells, maintaining healthy soil becomes essential. Implementing organic practices, such as cover cropping and mulching, can help improve soil structure, retain moisture, and enhance nutrient availability. These methods not only support rhubarb growth but also promote sustainable agriculture, ensuring that the land remains productive for future generations.

Irrigation strategies must also evolve in response to climate change. Traditional rain fed rhubarb cultivation may not suffice in regions experiencing reduced rainfall or prolonged drought. Growers are encouraged to adopt efficient irrigation systems that minimize water waste while ensuring plants receive adequate moisture. Techniques such as drip irrigation can provide targeted watering that supports plant health without over saturating the soil, which can lead to root rot and other issues. By integrating modern irrigation solutions, rhubarb growers can adapt to the challenges posed by fluctuating weather patterns.

Lastly, educating consumers about the importance of local and seasonal produce can contribute to the overall resilience of rhubarb cultivation. By promoting awareness of the impact of climate change on food systems, those who enjoy rhubarb can make informed choices that support sustainable farming practices. Engaging with local farmers and participating in community supported agriculture (CSA) programs can foster a stronger connection to the land and the seasonal rhythms of food production. In this way, the culinary history of rhubarb can continue to flourish, even in the face of changing environmental conditions.

Chapter 12:

Rhubarb Recipes: A Culinary Collection

Sweet Rhubarb Desserts

Sweet rhubarb desserts have long been a cherished category in culinary traditions, celebrated for their unique balance of tartness and sweetness.

This vibrant plant, often grown in home gardens, is not only a culinary staple but also carries a deep historical narrative that intertwines with various cultures. Rhubarb, known for its striking red stalks and broad green leaves, has been utilized in desserts across the globe, transforming simple ingredients into delightful confections. As we delve into the world of sweet rhubarb desserts, we will explore recipes, historical significance, and the evolution of this remarkable ingredient in the dessert landscape.

Historically, rhubarb has roots that trace back to ancient civilizations in China, where it was valued not just for its culinary qualities but also for its medicinal properties. The plant made its way to Europe in the 17th century, where it quickly gained popularity among cooks. By the 19th century, sweetened rhubarb desserts began to emerge, with recipes for pies, crumbles, and tarts becoming common in households. These desserts often blended the tart flavor of rhubarb with sugars, spices, and other fruits, showcasing the versatility of this unique ingredient. The historical journey of rhubarb serves as a testament to its adaptability, illustrating how cultures have embraced and transformed its use in sweet applications.

In contemporary cooking, rhubarb desserts can be found in various forms, from classic rhubarb pies to more innovative dishes like rhubarb sorbet or rhubarb infused cake. One popular dessert is the rhubarb crisp, which combines rhubarb with a crunchy topping made from oats, flour, and brown sugar, providing a delightful contrast in textures. Additionally, the combination of rhubarb with strawberries has become iconic, leading to the beloved strawberry rhubarb pie, a staple in many American households during spring and summer months. These desserts not only celebrate the seasonal availability of rhubarb but also highlight the importance of regional varieties and their unique flavors.

Rhubarb's tartness pairs beautifully with a variety of sweeteners and flavors, making it an excellent candidate for experimentation in dessert recipes. Honey, maple syrup, and brown sugar can enhance its natural sweetness, while spices like ginger and cinnamon add warmth and depth. Furthermore, incorporating complementary ingredients such as vanilla, citrus, or nuts can elevate rhubarb desserts, creating a symphony of flavors that delight the palate. As chefs and home bakers continue to explore new culinary landscapes, rhubarb remains a versatile ingredient that encourages creativity in sweet dishes.

As we embrace the role of rhubarb in seasonal cooking, it becomes evident that this extraordinary plant is not just a fleeting ingredient but one that has a rich narrative and a promising future in gastronomy. Celebrated in festivals and local markets, rhubarb invites communities to come together and appreciate its flavors through shared recipes and traditions. Whether enjoyed in a classic pie or a modern dessert, sweet rhubarb creations continue to captivate food enthusiasts, bridging the gap between history and contemporary culinary practices. Through this exploration of sweet rhubarb desserts, we honor the past while looking forward to the future possibilities of this remarkable ingredient.

Savory Rhubarb Dishes

Savory rhubarb dishes offer a delightful twist on the traditional sweet applications of this unique plant. While rhubarb is often celebrated for its tartness in desserts, its potential as a savory ingredient is gaining recognition among chefs and home cooks alike. Historically, rhubarb has been cultivated not just for its stalks but also for its versatility in various culinary traditions. The ancient use of rhubarb in Asian medicine and cuisine laid the groundwork for its incorporation into savory dishes, showcasing its adaptability beyond the dessert table.

One of the most traditional savory applications of rhubarb can be traced back to British cuisine, where it is often used in sauces that accompany roasted meats. The tangy flavor of rhubarb complements rich proteins, providing a refreshing contrast that elevates the dish. For instance, a rhubarb and ginger chutney can enhance the flavors of grilled lamb or pork, while a simple rhubarb compote can serve as an excellent condiment for poultry. These dishes not only highlight the tartness of rhubarb but also its ability to balance out heavier flavors, making it an essential ingredient in seasonal cooking.

In various cultures, rhubarb has been utilized in savory recipes that reflect local culinary practices. In Eastern Europe, for example, rhubarb is often included in stews and soups, where its acidity can brighten the overall flavor profile. This practice ties back to historical cultivation methods, where rhubarb was valued for its ability to thrive in cooler climates, making it a staple in regions with short growing seasons. The incorporation of rhubarb into savory dishes can be seen as a testament to the ingenuity of cooks who sought to maximize the use of available ingredients, ensuring nothing went to waste.

Modern gastronomy has also embraced the potential of rhubarb in savory cooking. Chefs are experimenting with pickled rhubarb, using it as a zesty garnish for salads and grain bowls. The natural acidity of rhubarb enhances the freshness of vegetables, while its vibrant color adds visual appeal to any dish. Additionally, pairing rhubarb with complementary flavors, such as fatty fish or earthy root vegetables, can create a harmonious balance on the plate. This evolution of rhubarb recipes showcases the ingredient's versatility, encouraging home cooks to think outside the box.

As rhubarb continues to gain popularity in contemporary cuisine, understanding its historical and cultural significance can enrich the culinary experience. Exploring savory rhubarb dishes allows us to appreciate the plant not only as a seasonal delight but as a bridge connecting various culinary traditions. Whether you are inspired by historical recipes or modern interpretations, incorporating savory rhubarb into your cooking can open up new flavor possibilities and celebrate this remarkable ingredient in a fresh way.

Preserved Rhubarb Delights

Rhubarb, often heralded as a perennial favorite in kitchens around the world, offers a unique tangy flavor that lends itself beautifully to preservation techniques. Traditionally, rhubarb has been enjoyed in various forms, from jams and jellies to pickles and sauces. The preservation of rhubarb not only extends its shelf life but also enhances its culinary versatility, allowing home cooks and chefs alike to incorporate this vibrant vegetable into their recipes year round. As we delve into the delights of preserved rhubarb, we will explore both historical methods and modern practices that continue to celebrate this remarkable ingredient.

Historically, the preservation of rhubarb can be traced back to ancient cultures that recognized its potential for both culinary and medicinal uses. In regions with cooler climates, where rhubarb thrives, people developed methods such as drying, canning, and fermenting to ensure they could enjoy its flavors long after the harvest season. These practices often stemmed from a need to make the most of a bountiful crop, as well as a desire to harness the plant's reputed health benefits. For instance, in traditional medicine, rhubarb has been used to aid digestion and detoxify the body, further encouraging its preservation for nutritional purposes.

As we enter the modern kitchen, the preservation techniques for rhubarb have evolved but remain rooted in these historical practices. Canning has become a popular method, allowing for the creation of rhubarb preserves that capture the essence of spring in a jar. Simple recipes for rhubarb jam typically involve combining the chopped rhubarb with sugar and lemon juice, simmering until thickened, and then canning in sterilized jars. This process not only retains the vibrant color and tart flavor of rhubarb but also makes it a delightful addition to breakfast spreads, desserts, and even savory dishes.

Freezing is another effective method for preserving rhubarb, offering a convenient option for those who prefer to maintain the fruit's fresh taste. By blanching the rhubarb stalks before freezing, cooks can prevent the loss of texture and flavor. Once frozen, rhubarb can be stored for months, making it accessible for pies, sauces, and smoothies even in the dead of winter. This versatility allows home cooks to experiment with rhubarb in various culinary contexts, proving that with proper preservation, the tangy delight of rhubarb can be enjoyed in countless ways.

In addition to its preservation methods, it's essential to consider how preserved rhubarb can be incorporated into modern gastronomy. Chefs are increasingly finding innovative ways to use preserved rhubarb to enhance dishes, from glazes for meats to components in salads and desserts. By pairing preserved rhubarb with complementary flavors such as ginger, vanilla, or citrus, culinary enthusiasts can create stunning presentations that celebrate this unique vegetable. As we embrace the art of preserving rhubarb, we not only honor its rich history but also open the door to new culinary adventures that will delight palates for generations to come.

Appendix: Rhubarb: A Botanical and Historical Overview Rhubarb's Botanical Profile Plant Classification: Explore the botanical family of rhubarb and its relationship to other plants. Cultivation and Growth: Learn about the optimal growing conditions for rhubarb, including soil requirements, planting, and care. Harvesting and Storage: Discover the best time to harvest rhubarb and how to store it for optimal freshness.

Rhubarb Through History Ancient Origins: Explore the historical use of rhubarb in different cultures. Rhubarb in Medicine: Discover the medicinal properties attributed to rhubarb throughout history. Rhubarb in Culinary Traditions: Explore the evolution of rhubarb in various cuisines around the world. Rhubarb Nutrition Nutritional Value: Understand the vitamins, minerals, and antioxidants found in rhubarb. Health Benefits: Explore the potential health benefits associated with rhubarb consumption.

Precautions: Learn about the oxalic acid content in rhubarb and safe consumption guidelines. Rhubarb in the Garden Companion Planting: Discover plants that complement rhubarb's growth. Pest and Disease Management: Learn how to protect your rhubarb plants from common problems. Rhubarb Varieties: Explore different rhubarb cultivars and their characteristics. By understanding the botanical and historical aspects of rhubarb, you can deepen your appreciation for this versatile ingredient and cultivate a thriving rhubarb patch.

Disclaimer: The information provided in this appendix is intended for informational purposes only and should not be considered as professional horticultural or medical advice. Always consult with a qualified expert for specific gardening or health related concerns. This document is intended for informational purposes only and does not constitute advice or endorsement of any specific products or services.

THE RHUBARB COOKBOOK

MASTERING COOKING TECHNIQUES AND STORAGE TIPS

Chapter 1:

Introduction to Rhubarb

The History of Rhubarb

Rhubarb has a rich and fascinating history that spans centuries and continents, making it a unique ingredient in the culinary world. Originally native to the regions of Asia, particularly in China, rhubarb was first cultivated for its medicinal properties rather than its culinary potential. Ancient Chinese medicine revered the plant for its laxative qualities and used it to treat various ailments. It wasn't until the 18th century that rhubarb began to gain popularity in Europe, particularly in England, where it was introduced as a garden plant and later embraced for its tart flavor in desserts and preserves.

The cultivation of rhubarb in Europe can be traced back to the late 17th century when it was brought over through trade routes. By the 18th century, it became a staple in British gardens, and its use expanded from medicinal purposes to culinary applications. English cooks began experimenting with rhubarb in pies, crumbles, and jams, highlighting its distinctive tartness and versatility. The plant flourished in the cooler climates of the north, particularly in Yorkshire, which became known as the "Rhubarb Triangle," a region famous for producing some of the finest rhubarb in the world.

As rhubarb's popularity grew, it began to appear in international cuisines, showcasing its adaptability and appeal across cultures. In Scandinavian countries, for instance, rhubarb was incorporated into traditional desserts and preserves, while in India, it found its way into savory dishes and chutneys. This cross cultural exchange of culinary practices not only diversified the ways rhubarb was used but also solidified its status as a beloved ingredient globally. From sweet to savory, the plant's unique flavor profile allowed chefs to experiment with rhubarb in innovative ways, leading to the creation of dishes that are now staples in many kitchens.

In contemporary cuisine, rhubarb continues to capture the attention of food enthusiasts, particularly in the realm of desserts. From classic rhubarb pies to modern takes on crumbles and cakes, the vibrant stalks lend themselves beautifully to sweet applications. Beyond desserts, chefs are increasingly recognizing rhubarb's potential in savory dishes, pairing it with proteins and seasonal vegetables to create a delightful contrast of flavors. Moreover, the rise of health conscious eating has spotlighted rhubarb for its nutritional benefits, encouraging home cooks to incorporate it into their diets in various forms, including beverages and preserves.

The modern resurgence of interest in rhubarb can also be attributed to its versatility in accommodating various dietary preferences, including gluten free options. With the increasing demand for gluten free recipes, rhubarb easily adapts to these culinary needs, allowing everyone to enjoy its delightful taste. As we explore the history and uses of rhubarb, it is clear that this fascinating plant is more than just a garden curiosity; it is a versatile ingredient that continues to inspire creativity in kitchens around the world. Whether you are crafting a classic dessert, infusing a cocktail, or preparing a savory dish, rhubarb remains a cherished component of the culinary landscape, inviting both seasoned chefs and home cooks alike to master its unique flavors.

Nutritional Benefits of Rhubarb

Rhubarb, often recognized for its vibrant color and tart flavor, is more than just a culinary delight; it is also a powerhouse of nutrition. This unique plant, often mistaken for a fruit, is packed with vitamins, minerals, and antioxidants that contribute to a healthy diet. One of the most notable benefits of rhubarb is its high content of dietary fiber, which aids in digestion and promotes a feeling of fullness. Including fiber rich foods in your meals can support weight management and overall digestive health, making rhubarb an excellent addition to various recipes, from desserts to savory dishes.

In addition to fiber, rhubarb is low in calories, making it an appealing choice for those looking to maintain a healthy diet without compromising on flavor. A cup of cooked rhubarb contains roughly 26 calories, allowing you to enjoy its tangy taste while keeping your calorie intake in check. This low calorie profile makes rhubarb an ideal ingredient for creating guilt free desserts, such as pies and crumbles, as well as refreshing beverages like smoothies and cocktails. By incorporating rhubarb into your meals, you can indulge in delicious flavors while supporting your nutritional goals.

Rhubarb is also rich in essential vitamins and minerals, particularly vitamin K, which plays a crucial role in bone health and blood clotting. Furthermore, it contains decent amounts of vitamin C, which is important for immune function and skin health. The presence of antioxidants, such as anthocyanin, adds to rhubarb's health benefits by fighting free radicals in the body and reducing inflammation. This makes rhubarb not only a tasty addition to your favorite recipes but also a beneficial one for your overall well being.

For those interested in exploring rhubarb's versatility in cooking, its nutritional profile offers numerous opportunities for creative culinary applications. Savory dishes featuring rhubarb can be paired with proteins like chicken or pork, creating a unique flavor contrast that enhances the meal. Additionally, rhubarb can be combined with seasonal produce, like strawberries or asparagus, to elevate the nutritional value of your dishes. This not only adds depth to your meals but also encourages the consumption of a variety of nutrients essential for good health.

Finally, rhubarb is an excellent ingredient for those with specific dietary needs, such as gluten free diets. Its natural properties lend themselves well to developing recipes that cater to various preferences without sacrificing taste or texture. From wholesome preserves to delightful desserts and beverages, rhubarb can be adapted to suit anyone's palate. By embracing the nutritional benefits of rhubarb, you can enjoy a delicious and health conscious approach to cooking that delights the senses and nourishes the body.

Selecting and Storing Rhubarb

The Rhubarb Cookbook: Mastering Cooking Techniques and Storage Tips

Selecting and storing rhubarb is an essential skill for anyone looking to incorporate this vibrant, tart vegetable into their culinary repertoire. When selecting rhubarb, look for firm, crisp stalks that are free of blemishes or signs of wilting. The color can range from deep red to a more muted green, depending on the variety, but the most important factor is the texture; stalks should feel solid and have a slight sheen. Avoid stalks that are excessively thin or have a fibrous appearance, as these can affect the quality of your dishes. Fresh rhubarb will have a bright appearance, indicating that it has been recently harvested and will deliver the best flavor and texture in your recipes.

Once you have selected your rhubarb, proper storage is crucial to maintain its freshness. If you plan to use the rhubarb within a few days, simply wrap the stalks in a damp paper towel and place them in a perforated plastic bag in the vegetable crisper of your refrigerator. This method helps maintain moisture while allowing for air circulation, which is key to preventing spoilage. When stored correctly, fresh rhubarb can last for up to a week, giving you ample time to experiment with various rhubarb recipes, from classic pies and crumbles to savory dishes and refreshing beverages.

For those looking to extend the life of their rhubarb beyond its fresh state, freezing is an excellent option. To freeze rhubarb, start by washing and trimming the stalks, then slice them into manageable pieces. Blanching the chopped rhubarb in boiling water for just one to two minutes before plunging it into ice water will help preserve its vibrant color and flavor. Once cooled, drain the pieces thoroughly and spread them on a baking sheet to freeze individually before transferring them to airtight containers or freezer bags. Properly frozen rhubarb can last for up to a year, allowing for year round enjoyment in your favorite rhubarb desserts and preserves.

When it comes to using stored rhubarb, it's important to remember that frozen rhubarb may release more moisture during cooking than fresh stalks. Adjusting your recipes to account for this extra moisture ensures that your pies, crumbles, and savory dishes maintain the desired texture. Additionally, frozen rhubarb is perfect for blending into smoothies or crafting unique cocktails, where its tart flavor can shine without the need for extensive cooking. Embrace the versatility of rhubarb, and let the seasonality of this ingredient inspire your culinary creations.

In summary, selecting the right rhubarb and mastering its storage can significantly elevate your cooking and baking endeavors.

Whether you're embracing its tartness in a refreshing drink, crafting a decadent dessert, or exploring savory dishes, the key to achieving the best results starts with quality ingredients and thoughtful preservation techniques. By implementing these tips, you can ensure that rhubarb remains a staple in your kitchen, ready to complement seasonal produce and bring a unique twist to a variety of dishes.

Chapter 2:

Rhubarb Cooking Techniques

Preparing Rhubarb

Preparing rhubarb is an essential step in unlocking its culinary potential, whether you're aiming to create a sweet pie, a savory dish, or a refreshing beverage. This unique vegetable, often treated as a fruit, boasts a tart flavor that can elevate a variety of recipes. Understanding how to properly prepare rhubarb will not only enhance your dishes but also ensure that the natural essence of this versatile ingredient shines through. With the right techniques, anyone from the novice home cook to the seasoned chef can appreciate the joys of working with rhubarb.

The first step in preparing rhubarb is selecting the right stalks. It's vital to choose firm, vibrant stalks that are free of blemishes or soft spots. When purchasing rhubarb, look for stalks that are bright red or pink, as these tend to be sweeter compared to their green counterparts. While both varieties can be used in cooking, the red stalks are generally preferred for desserts. Once you've selected your rhubarb, store it in the refrigerator wrapped in a damp paper towel to maintain its freshness until you're ready to use it.

Cleaning rhubarb is straightforward but crucial. Begin by rinsing the stalks under cold water to remove any dirt or debris. Avoid soaking them, as this can lead to waterlogging and diminish their flavor. After rinsing, trim off the leaves, which are toxic and should never be consumed. Cut the stalks into even pieces about one inch lengths are ideal for most recipes. The size of the pieces can affect cooking time, so uniformity is key to achieving even results in dishes like pies, crumbles, or savory mains.

Incorporating rhubarb into your cooking requires an understanding of its flavor profile. Due to its tartness, it is often paired with sweeteners, making it a favorite for desserts like rhubarb pie or crumbles. However, rhubarb also shines in savory dishes. Consider using it in sauces, as a unique side dish, or even in a salad to add a refreshing tang. Experimenting with rhubarb in ever ages can also yield exciting results; try blending it into smoothies or crafting a rhubarb infused cocktail for a refreshing twist.

Finally, mastering the art of cooking rhubarb involves knowing how to balance its tartness with other ingredients. For those looking to preserve rhubarb, canning it into jams or preserves can capture its flavor for enjoyment year round. When preparing gluten free dishes, rhubarb can be a fantastic ingredient that complements various gluten free flours in baked goods. As you explore the countless ways to incorporate rhubarb into your meals, remember that its versatility allows for creativity in both sweet and savory applications, making it a delightful addition to any culinary repertoire.

Cooking Methods for Rhubarb

Cooking methods for rhubarb are as diverse as the recipes it inspires, making it a versatile ingredient in both sweet and savory dishes. This unique vegetable, often mistaken for a fruit, adds a vibrant tartness that can elevate any meal. Understanding the various cooking techniques will not only enhance your culinary skills but also broaden your enjoyment of rhubarb in your kitchen. From traditional methods to modern innovations, mastering these techniques will allow you to create an array of dishes, from pies and crumbles to savory mains and refreshing beverages. One of the most common methods of preparing rhubarb is simmering. This technique is particularly useful when making desserts such as rhubarb compote or jams. To simmer rhubarb, simply chop it into small pieces and cook it slowly in a pot with a bit of water and sugar. The gentle heat helps to break down the fibrous texture, transforming the rhubarb into a soft, luscious filling for pies or a sweet topping for desserts. Simmering can also be adapted for savory dishes, where the tartness of the rhubarb complements meats and vegetables, providing a refreshing counterpoint.

Roasting is another exciting method to explore. This technique not only intensifies the flavors of rhubarb but also enhances its natural sweetness. When roasted, rhubarb caramelizes, creating a delightful contrast between its tartness and the rich, deep flavors that emerge. Simply toss rhubarb with a bit of oil and seasoning, then roast in the oven until tender. This method works beautifully in savory dishes, where roasted rhubarb can be paired with meats or served as a vibrant side dish, bringing a unique twist to your meal.

For those looking to incorporate rhubarb into beverages, juicing and blending are essential methods. Rhubarb can be juiced to create refreshing drinks or blended into smoothies for a nutritious boost. When preparing beverages, it's important to balance the tartness of rhubarb with other ingredients, such as sweet fruits or herbs. This not only makes the drinks more palatable but also highlights the fresh, tangy flavor of the rhubarb. Experimenting with cocktails or teas that feature rhubarb can lead t delightful discoveries, perfect for gatherings or a quiet evening at home.

Finally, preserving rhubarb through canning or making jams is a wonderful way to enjoy its flavor year round. Proper techniques include sterilizing jars and ensuring the correct sugar to rhubarb ratio to create a product that is both safe and delicious. The process of making preserves allows for creativity, where you can add spices or other fruits to enhance the flavor profile. Whether you are making a classic rhubarb jam or experimenting with seasonal produce pairings, mastering these preservation methods will ensure you have a stock of rhubarb treats to enjoy long after its season has ended. By exploring these cooking methods, you can fully embrace the versatility of rhubarb in your culinary adventures.

Pairing Rhubarb with Other Ingredients

Pairing rhubarb with complementary ingredients can elevate its unique tartness and enhance the overall flavor profile of any dish. This vibrant vegetable, often mistaken for fruit, boasts a distinct acidity that can cut through rich flavors, making it an excellent addition to both sweet and savory recipes. When considering how to pair rhubarb, it's essential to explore a variety of ingredients that balance its sharpness, whether you're crafting a dessert, a main course, or even a refreshing beverage.

In the realm of desserts, rhubarb shines brightly when combined with sweet fruits such as strawberries, apples, or pears. The natural sweetness of these fruits can help mellow rhubarb's tartness, creating a harmonious blend perfect for pies, crumbles, and cakes. Classic combinations, like rhubarb strawberry pie, highlight how these two ingredients can work in concert to deliver a delightful balance of flavors. For a modern twist, consider adding spices like ginger or cardamom to enhance the depth of your desserts, or try incorporating citrus elements, such as orange zest, to brighten the dish and add an exciting layer of flavor.

When venturing into savory territory, rhubarb can be a surprising yet delicious addition to main courses and side dishes. Its tartness can complement richer proteins like pork, duck, or lamb, offering a refreshing contrast that enhances the overall meal experience. Pairing rhubarb with seasonal vegetables such as asparagus or green beans can also yield delightful results. A rhubarb salsa, for instance, can add a zesty kick to grilled meats, while a rhubarb chutney can serve as a perfect accompaniment to cheese platters or charcuterie boards, showcasing the versatility of this often underappreciated ingredient.

For those looking to create refreshing beverages, rhubarb can be infused into cocktails, smoothies, and teas, imparting its distinct tartness and vibrant color. Combining rhubarb with ingredients like ginger, mint, or citrus can create invigorating drinks that are perfect for any occasion. A rhubarb cocktail, for example, can be crafted by muddling fresh rhubarb with spirits and a splash of soda, resulting in a refreshing and visually appealing drink. Additionally, rhubarb can be incorporated into homemade syrups for use in various beverages, offering a unique twist that will impress guests and keep them coming back for more. Lastly, the art of preserving rhubarb opens up even more opportunities for delightful pairings. By canning rhubarb into jams or preserves, you can create spreads that marry its tartness with the sweetness of sugar or honey, as well as other fruits like raspberries or blueberries. This not only allows you to enjoy rhubarb year round but also makes it a versatile ingredient for breakfast items, desserts, or even savory dishes. For those adhering to gluten free diets, experimenting with gluten free flours in rhubarb recipes can yield equally delicious results without sacrificing flavor or texture. With a little creativity, the possibilities for pairing rhubarb with other ingredients are virtually endless, inviting you to explore new culinary horizons.

Chapter 3:

Rhubarb Recipes

Rhubarb Desserts

Rhubarb desserts hold a special place in the pantheon of sweet treats, celebrated for their unique tartness and versatility. As a key ingredient, rhubarb transforms classic desserts into delightful confections, balancing sweetness with its unmistakable tang. From pies that evoke nostalgia to crumbles that offer a comforting crunch, rhubarb desserts are a testament to the ingredient's adaptability. This chapter explores various dessert options, emphasizing techniques and tips to master the art of cooking with this vibrant vegetable.

One of the most beloved ways to enjoy rhubarb is in pies. A traditional rhubarb pie showcases the fruit's natural tartness, often enhanced with sugar and spices like cinnamon and nutmeg. The process begins with selecting the freshest rhubarb, ensuring that the stalks are firm and vibrant in color. Preparing the filling involves chopping the rhubarb and combining it with sugar, which helps to draw out moisture and flavor. Pairing rhubarb with strawberries or apples can create a harmonious blend, adding depth to the pie's flavor profile. A flaky, buttery crust envelops the filling, resulting in a dessert that is both comforting and refreshing.

Crumble desserts are another fantastic way to highlight rhubarb, offering a delightful texture contrast with their crunchy topping. The beauty of a rhubarb crumble lies in its simplicity; combining rhubarb with sugar and touch of lemon juice creates a bright, flavorful base. The topping, made from a mixture of oats, flour, butter, and brown sugar, adds a satisfying crunch that complements the soft, tender rhubarb. This dessert is particularly appealing for those who appreciate a quick and easy preparation, as it requires minimal effort while delivering maximum flavor.

Rhubarb cakes introduce a delightful twist to traditional baking, allowing for innovative flavor combinations. A rhubarb upside down cake provides a stunning presentation, with caramelized rhubarb forming a beautiful base for a moist, tender cake. The tartness of the rhubarb pairs wonderfully with a sweet vanilla batter, creating a balanced dessert that is sure to impress. Additionally, incorporating rhubarb into muffins or coffee cakes offers an excellent way to enjoy this versatile ingredient, making it suitable for breakfast or afternoon tea. The incorporation of spices, nuts, or even chocolate can elevate these baked goods, making them a favorite among both casual bakers and seasoned pastry chefs.

For those who prefer gluten free options, rhubarb desserts can easily be adapted to accommodate dietary needs. By using gluten free flours or almond flour in place of traditional wheat flour, bakers can create delicious rhubarb pies, crumbles, and cakes that are accessible to everyone. Exploring alternative sweeteners and binding agents can also enhance the flavor while ensuring a satisfying texture. This inclusivity allows rhubarb lovers to enjoy their favorite desserts without compromising on taste or experience.

In conclusion, rhubarb desserts are not just a seasonal treat; they are an opportunity to explore flavors and textures that celebrate this unique ingredient. From classic pies and comforting crumbles to innovative cakes and gluten free adaptations, the possibilities are endless. Whether you are a seasoned baker or a curious novice, incorporating rhubarb into your dessert repertoire can bring a refreshing twist to your culinary creations. Embrace the tartness of rhubarb and let it inspire your next sweet endeavor, transforming your kitchen into a haven of delightful rhubarb infused indulgence.

Rhubarb Pies

Rhubarb pies are a delightful way to celebrate the unique tartness of this vibrant vegetable, often mistaken for fruit. This classic dessert showcases rhubarb's natural sourness, balanced perfectly with sugar and enveloped in a flaky, buttery crust. Whether you are using fresh rhubarb from your garden r frozen stalks, making a pie allows you to explore various flavor combinations and textures. The simplicity of pie making, combined with the complex flavors of rhubarb, makes it an accessible and rewarding experience for both novice and seasoned bakers alike.

To create the perfect rhubarb pie, it is essential to understand the balance of flavors. Rhubarb's tartness can be intense, so pairing it with sweeteners like ugar or honey is crucial. Commonly, recipes may call for additional fruits such as strawberries or apples to complement the rhubarb's acidity, creating a harmonious blend that enhances the overall taste. The addition of spices such as cinnamon or nutmeg can also elevate the flavor, adding warmth and depth to the filling. Experimenting with these combinations can lead to personalized recipes that reflect your taste preferences and showcase the versatility of rhubarb.

When preparing rhubarb for pie, selecting the right stalks is vital. Look for firm, bright red to pink stalks that are crisp and free from blemishes. Avoid any yellow or wilted stalks, as they may indicate over ripeness or poor quality. Once you have your rhubarb, it's important to wash and chop it properly. Some recipes recommend pre cooking the rhubarb briefly to soften it and reduce excess moisture, which prevents a soggy crust. This technique not only helps in achieving the ideal texture but also intensifies the flavors, making for a more robust pie filling.

The crust is another critical component of a successful rhubarb pie. A flaky, well prepared crust can elevate the dessert, providing a satisfying contrast to the soft and tangy filling. For those who are gluten free, there are numerous alternatives available, including almond flour or a gluten free all purpose blend. These substitutes can create a delicious and tender crust without compromising the integrity of the pie. Whether you choose to make your crust from scratch or opt for a store bought version, ensuring it is properly chilled and handled with care will yield the best results.

Rhubarb pies can be served in a variety of ways, from a simple slice enjoyed on its own to a more elaborate presentation with a scoop of vanilla ice cream or a dollop of whipped cream. These desserts not only satisfy a sweet tooth but also serve as a celebration of seasonal produce, allowing you to connect with the natural rhythms of the garden. Sharing a homemade rhubarb pie with family and friends can be a delightful experience, bringing people together over a dish that embodies the essence of spring and summer. As you explore the world of rhubarb pies, you'll discover that this unique ingredient offers endless possibilities for creativity and enjoyment in your kitchen.

Rhubarb Crumbles

Rhubarb crumbles are a quintessential dessert that beautifully showcases the unique tartness of rhubarb while providing a comforting and satisfying experience. This dessert combines the angry flavor of rhubarb with a sweet, buttery crumble topping, making it an irresistible option for any occasion. The beauty of rhubarb crumbles lies not only in their taste but also in their versatility; they can be enjoyed warm from the oven, served cold, or even paired with a scoop of ice cream for an indulgent treat. This section will delve into the techniques for creating perfect rhubarb crumbles, highlighting essential tips and variations that cater to a diverse range of dietary preferences and occasions.

To achieve the ideal crumble texture, selecting the right type of rhubarb is crucial. Look for Arm, vibrant stalks that are free from blemishes. When preparing the rhubarb, it is essential to wash and chop it into manageable pieces, ensuring even cooking. A typical crumble recipe will often include sugar to balance the tartness of the rhubarb, along with a splash of lemon juice or zest to enhance its natural flavors. To create a balanced filling, consider mixing rhubarb with other seasonal produce, such as strawberries or apples, which not only complements the tartness but also adds natural sweetness and texture.

The crumble topping is where creativity can truly shine. A classic crumble is made from a mixture of flour, butter, and sugar, but there are numerous variations to explore. For those following gluten free diets, substituting traditional flour with almond flour or gluten free oats can yield equally delicious results. For a healthier twist, consider incorporating nuts or seeds into the topping for added crunch and nutrition. Additionally, spices such as cinnamon or nutmeg can be added to the crumble mix, imparting warmth and depth to the Anal dish.

When it comes to baking, the ideal temperature and timing are key to achieving a golden brown topping while ensuring the rhubarb is tender and juicy. Typically, baking rhubarb crumbles at around 350°F (175°C) for 30 to 40 minutes will produce a delightful result. It is advisable to keep an eye on the crumble towards the end of the baking time; covering it with foil if it starts to brown too quickly can help maintain a perfect finish. Allowing the crumble to rest for a few minutes after removing it from the oven will also help the filling set, making it easier to serve.

Rhubarb crumbles are not just limited to traditional desserts; they can also be adapted into a variety of dishes that cater to different tastes and dietary needs. From vegan options using coconut oil instead of butter to innovative pairings with spices that reflect international cuisines, the possibilities are endless. Whether enjoyed as a simple family dessert or dressed up for a dinner party, rhubarb crumbles remain a beloved choice that highlights the vibrant flavors of this unique ingredient, making them a staple in any rhubarb enthusiast's repertoire.

Rhubarb Cakes

Rhubarb cakes are a delightful way to showcase the tartness of rhubarb while indulging in the rich textures and flavors that cakes can offer. These desserts provide a unique balance, combining sweetness with the tangy profile of rhubarb, making them a perfect treat for any occasion. The versatility of rhubarb allows it to be incorporated into various cake recipes, ranging from simple loaf cakes to more elaborate layered creations. In this subchapter, we will explore a variety of rhubarb cake recipes, emphasizing he techniques that enhance this unique ingredient's natural flavor.

One classic approach to rhubarb cakes is the rhubarb coffee cake, which pairs beautifully with a morning cup of coffee or tea. This cake typically features a moist, tender crumb, enhanced with diced rhubarb and topped with a crumbly streusel. The tartness of the rhubarb cuts through the sweetness of the cake, creating a delightful contrast that makes each bite satisfying. When preparing this cake, it is essential to choose fresh rhubarb with firm stalks, as it will provide the best flavor and texture. Incorporating spices like cinnamon or nutmeg can further elevate the cake, adding warmth and depth to the overall taste.

For those who enjoy experimenting with flavors, a rhubarb upside down cake is an exciting option. This cake showcases the rhubarb in an eye catching presentation, with the fruit caramelized at the bottom, creating a beautiful display when inverted. The technique involves layering rhubarb slices in a caramel sauce before pouring the cake batter over the top. As it bakes, the rhubarb infuses the cake with its tartness while also adding moisture. This recipe is an excellent way to impress guests at gatherings, as its stunning appearance and delicious flavor combination make it a standout dessert.

In addition to traditional cakes, gluten free rhubarb options have gained popularity, allowing those with dietary restrictions to enjoy this delightful fruit. Almond flour or a gluten free all purpose blend can be used to create a light and airy cake that does not compromise on flavor. Incorporating ingredients like yogurt or sour cream can also enhance the cake's moisture while providing a tangy note that complements the rhubarb. These gluten free rhubarb cakes are not only accessible but also delicious, ensuring that everyone can partake in the joy of baking with rhubarb.

Finally, rhubarb cakes can be a family friendly endeavor, perfect for involving children in the kitchen. Simple recipes that allow for hands on participation, such as mixing, pouring, and decorating, can make baking with rhubarb a fun activity. For example, a rhubarb cupcake recipe allows kids to enjoy the process of baking while creating individual servings. Topped with a light frosting or a dusting of powdered sugar, these cupcakes can be a delightful treat that children will love. By making rhubarb cakes an engaging family activity, you can foster a love for cooking and instill an appreciation for this unique ingredient in the next generation.

Savory Rhubarb Dishes

Savory rhubarb dishes offer a delightful twist to the conventional perception of this tart vegetable, often relegated to sweet desserts. While many are familiar with rhubarb's role in pies and crumbles, its unique flavor profile can elevate a variety of savory dishes. The tangy notes of rhubarb can enhance rich meats, brighten up vegetable medleys, and even add an unexpected zing to sauces and dressings. This subchapter explores how to incorporate rhubarb into main courses and side dishes, showcasing its versatility and encouraging culinary creativity.

One captivating way to use rhubarb is in savory sauces that accompany meats. A rhubarb and ginger sauce, for example, can be paired with grilled chicken or pork, creating a harmonious balance between the meat's richness and the sauce's tangy sweetness. To prepare this sauce, simmer diced rhubarb with fresh ginger, garlic, and a splash of vinegar until the rhubarb softens. This mixture can then be blended to achieve a smooth consistency, offering a vibrant complement to your main dish. The key is to adjust the sweetness and acidity to suit your palate, ensuring that the sauce enhances rather than overpowers the protein.

In addition to sauces, rhubarb can play a starring role in vegetable dishes. A rhubarb and asparagus stir fry is a fresh and zesty side that celebrates seasonal produce. Start by sautéing asparagus in olive oil, then add chopped rhubarb for the final few minutes of cooking. The rhubarb will soften slightly but retain its structure, lending a pleasant tartness that contrasts beautifully with the tender asparagus. Finish with a sprinkle of sesame seeds and a drizzle of soy sauce for a dish that is not only colorful but also packed with flavor.

Rhubarb can also be incorporated into grain based dishes, such as salads or pilafs. A quinoa salad featuring roasted rhubarb, nuts, and feta cheese provides a delightful mix of textures and tastes. Roast the rhubarb until it caramelizes slightly, which mellows its tartness, then toss it with cooked quinoa, toasted almonds, and crumbled feta. The result is a refreshing and nutritious dish that can be served warm or chilled, making it a perfect addition to any meal or as a standalone lunch option.

Lastly, rhubarb's integration into international cuisines showcases its adaptability. In Indian cooking, for instance, rhubarb can be used to create a unique chutney, blending it with spices like cumin, mustard seeds, and chili peppers. This chutney serves as a vibrant accompaniment to curries and flatbreads, introducing a distinct flavor that elevates traditional dishes. By exploring different cultural applications of rhubarb, home cooks can discover new ways to appreciate this often overlooked ingredient, offering both familiar comfort and exciting new tastes.

Incorporating rhubarb into savory dishes not only highlights its versatility but also invites experimentation in the kitchen. From sauces and sides to salads and international flavors, the possibilities are endless. As you explore these savory rhubarb dishes, remember that the key is to balance its tartness with other ingredients, allowing this vibrant vegetable to shine in every bite. Embrace the challenge of using rhubarb in unexpected ways, and you'll uncover a treasure trove of unique and delicious meals that will impress family and friends alike.

Main Courses with Rhubarb

Rhubarb is often celebrated for its role in desserts, but its unique tartness and vibrant color can elevate savory dishes as well. Incorporating rhubarb into main courses adds a refreshing twist, balancing flavors and creating unexpected culinary experiences. From savory stews to roasted meats, rhubarb can enhance the complexity of a dish, making it an exciting ingredient for those looking to experiment in the kitchen.

One of the most delightful ways to use rhubarb in savory cooking is by creating a rhubarb chutney. This condiment pairs beautifully with roasted meats, particularly pork and chicken. The tartness of the rhubarb complements the richness of the meat, while spices like ginger and cinnamon add depth. This chutney can be prepared in advance and stored in jars, making it a convenient option for quick weeknight dinners or special gatherings. The combination of sweet and sour flavors not only enhances the main course but also provides a beautiful contrast on the plate.

Another innovative approach is to incorporate rhubarb into grain based dishes. For example, a rhubarb infused quinoa salad can serve as a delightful main course or a hearty side. By cooking the quinoa in a rhubarb broth, you impart a subtle tang that enhances the nutty flavor of the grain. Tossing in roasted vegetables and a zesty vinaigrette will create a well rounded dish that showcases rhubarb's versatility. This method not only introduces a new flavor profile but also offers a nutritious option for gluten free diets, appealing to a broader audience.

Rhubarb can also be featured in braised dishes, where its acidity helps tenderize meats while imparting a distinct flavor. A braised lamb shank with rhubarb and herbs creates a comforting and hearty meal. The slow cooking process allows the rhubarb to break down, melding its tartness with the rich flavors of the lamb. This technique opens up a world of possibilities, as you can experiment with various meats and additional ingredients, such as root vegetables, to create a satisfying and balanced main course.

In addition to its culinary applications, rhubarb also offers several health benefits, making it an excellent choice for those conscious of their diet. Rich in vitamins K and C, as well as dietary fiber, rhubarb can contribute to overall wellness while adding a unique flavor to main courses. By embracing rhubarb in savory dishes, cooks can tap into its nutritional value while exploring new culinary horizons. Whether you're a seasoned chef or a home cook eager to try something new, incorporating rhubarb into main courses promises to be a rewarding adventure for any food lover.

Side Dishes Featuring Rhubarb

Side dishes featuring rhubarb offer a delightful way to elevate your meals, showcasing its unique tartness and versatility. While rhubarb is often celebrated for its role in desserts, its flavor profile can also enhance savory dishes, making it an excellent companion to a variety of ingredients. This subchapter will explore several delicious side dish ideas that incorporate rhubarb, providing inspiration for anyone looking to expand their culinary repertoire and impress guests with innovative flavors.

One of the most refreshing side dishes you can create with rhubarb is a rhubarb and asparagus salad. The bright tartness of rhubarb pairs beautifully with the earthy, slightly sweet notes of asparagus, creating a balanced dish that can be served warm or cold. To make this salad, lightly salute chopped rhubarb and asparagus in olive oil, then toss them with toasted almonds and a zesty lemon vinaigrette. This combination not only highlights the seasonal produce but also offers a colorful presentation that is sure to catch the eye on any dining table.

For a heartier side dish, consider preparing a rhubarb and potato gratin. Layer thinly sliced potatoes with sautéed onions and rhubarb, and cover the mixture with a creamy béchamel sauce, seasoned with fresh herbs like thyme or rosemary. As it bakes, the rhubarb's natural acidity cuts through the richness of the cream, creating a beautifully balanced dish that harmonizes flavors and textures. This gratin makes an excellent accompaniment to roasted meats or grilled Ash, adding an unexpected twist to your meal.

Rhubarb also shines in vegetable stir fries, where its tangy flavor can enliven a variety of seasonal vegetables. Incorporate rhubarb into a stir fry with bell peppers, snap peas, and carrots for a vibrant and colorful dish. The key is to slice the rhubarb into thin strips and add it towards the end of cooking, allowing it to soften slightly while retaining a bit of its crunch. A splash of soy sauce, sesame oil, and a sprinkle of sesame seeds will enhance the dish, bringing together the sweet and savory elements for a delightful side. Finally, rhubarb can be transformed into a vibrant chutney that pairs beautifully with grilled meats, cheese platters, or as a spread for sandwiches. Cook diced rhubarb with onions, ginger, vinegar, and a touch of sugar until it thickens into a chunky condiment. This chutney captures the essence of rhubarb's tartness, making it an excellent counterpoint to richer flavors. Whether served warm or chilled, it adds a unique touch to any meal, showcasing the versatility of rhubarb beyond the realm of sweets.

In summary, rhubarb is an underutilized ingredient in savory side dishes that can add depth and interest to your meals. From salads and gratins to stir fries and chutneys, the possibilities are endless. By incorporating rhubarb into your cooking, you not only embrace its flavor but also enhance your culinary creativity, allowing you to impress family and friends with dishes that are both unique and delicious.

Rhubarb Beverages

Rhubarb is often celebrated for its versatility in the kitchen, but its potential extends far beyond pies and crumbles. One of the most delightful ways to harness the vibrant, tangy flavor of rhubarb is through beverages. From refreshing cocktails to invigorating smoothies and soothing teas, rhubarb beverages offer an exciting and dynamic way to enjoy this unique ingredient. This subchapter delves into the art of crafting drinks that elevate rhubarb's natural tartness, making it a staple in any beverage repertoire.

One popular option is the rhubarb cocktail, which can be as simple or as complex as one desires. A rhubarb infused gin and tonic, for instance, showcases the tartness of the rhubarb while harmonizing beautifully with the botanicals of the gin. To create this refreshing drink, you can prepare a rhubarb syrup by simmering chopped rhubarb with sugar and water until it reaches a syrupy consistency. This syrup can then be mixed with gin, tonic water, and a squeeze of fresh lime for a delightful twist on a classic drink. For those interested in experimenting further, consider adding herbs like basil or mint to enhance the flavor profile.

Smoothies are another fantastic way to incorporate rhubarb into your beverage routine. The tangy flavor of rhubarb pairs wonderfully with a variety of fruits, such as strawberries, bananas, or apples. A delightful rhubarb strawberry smoothie can be made by blending fresh or frozen rhubarb and strawberries with yogurt or a plant based milk for a creamy texture. This not only makes for a delicious drink but also packs a nutritional punch, offering vitamins and fiber that support a healthy diet. Adjusting the sweetness with honey or agave syrup allows for customization according to personal taste preferences.

For those seeking a warm and comforting option, rhubarb tea is a soothing choice. This can be made by steeping dried rhubarb leaves or using rhubarb stalks in hot water, creating a subtly tart infusion. Adding honey or a splash of lemon can enhance the flavor while providing a delightful aroma. Rhubarb tea can be enjoyed on its own or blended with other herbal teas, such as chamomile or ginger, for added complexity. This beverage not only warms the soul but also showcases rhubarb's ability to shine in both hot and cold formats.

In addition to conventional beverages, rhubarb can also be used creatively in homemade sodas and sparkling drinks. By combining rhubarb syrup with sparkling water or soda, you can create a refreshing, non alcoholic drink that is perfect for warm days or gatherings. Adding a dash of bitters can introduce an intriguing layer of flavor, making it suitable for both children and adults. The vibrant pink hue of rhubarb based drinks adds a visual appeal that makes any occasion feel special.

In conclusion, rhubarb beverages offer an exciting avenue for exploration beyond traditional cooking. Whether crafting a cocktail, blending a smoothie, or steeping a soothing tea, the tartness of rhubarb can enhance a wide array of drinks. These beverages not only celebrate rhubarb's unique flavor but also provide opportunities for creativity and customization, allowing anyone who enjoys food and rhubarb to experiment and And their perfect sip.

Cocktails

Cocktails have long been a favorite way to celebrate flavors, and when it comes to incorporating rhubarb, the possibilities are both exciting and refreshing. Rhubarb's natural tartness adds an intriguing depth to a variety of beverages, making it a perfect candidate for cocktails that stand out. This subchapter explores various rhubarb based cocktails, showcasing how this unique ingredient can elevate your drink game and impress guests at any gathering.

To start, consider the classic Rhubarb Fizz, which combines rhubarb syrup with gin and a splash of tonic water. The syrup is made by simmering rhubarb with sugar and a hint of lemon juice until it transforms into a vibrant, fragrant liquid. This not only provides a sweet balance to the gin's botanical notes but also brings a beautiful blush color to the drink. Garnishing with a sprig of fresh mint or a slice of lemon adds a visual appeal and a refreshing aroma, making it a delightful choice for spring and summer gatherings.

For those who enjoy a more complex flavor profile, the Rhubarb and Elderflower Collins offers an elegant twist. This cocktail marries the tartness of rhubarb with the floral notes of elderflower liqueur, creating a harmonious blend that is both refreshing and sophisticated. By mixing rhubarb puree with fresh lemon juice, elderflower liqueur, and soda water, you can serve up a drink that is not only delicious but also visually stunning. A garnish of edible flowers can enhance the presentation, making it a perfect choice for special occasions or brunch.

If you're looking for a non alcoholic option, rhubarb can also shine in mocktails. A Rhubarb Lemonade combines homemade rhubarb syrup with fresh lemon juice and sparkling water, resulting in a bubbly, thirst quenching beverage that everyone can enjoy. This drink is not just a way to cool down on a hot day; it also highlights rhubarb's versatility and ability to complement other flavors, making it a great addition to family gatherings or picnics.

Lastly, experimenting with rhubarb in cocktails allows for endless creativity Consider pairing rhubarb with seasonal fruits like strawberries or blueberries, or even herbs like basil and thyme, to craft unique flavor combinations. This encourages exploration and innovation, inviting anyone who enjoys food and rhubarb to discover new favorites. With the right techniques and a bit of imagination, rhubarb cocktails can become a staple in your beverage repertoire, offering a delightful way to celebrate this tangy ingredient.

Smoothies

Smoothies are a delightful way to incorporate rhubarb into your daily routine, offering a refreshing and nutritious option that can be enjoyed any time of day. With its tart flavor, rhubarb adds a unique twist to traditional smoothie recipes, creating a vibrant drink that not only tastes great but also packs a nutritional punch.

By blending rhubarb with a variety of fruits, vegetables, and other ingredients, you can elevate your smoothie game while reaping the health benefits that this versatile vegetable has to offer.

When preparing rhubarb smoothies, it's essential to balance its tartness with sweeter fruits. Strawberries, bananas, and apples are excellent companions, softening rhubarb's sharp flavor while enhancing the overall taste. To prepare rhubarb for smoothies, it's advisable to cook it briefly, either by steaming or simmering, to mellow its acidity and soften its texture. This step not only makes the rhubarb easier to blend but also enriches the smoothie with a deeper flavor profile. For those looking for a refreshing summer drink, consider combining cooked rhubarb with fresh mint, yogurt, and a splash of honey for sweetness.

In addition to fruits, incorporating leafy greens can boost the nutritional value of your rhubarb smoothie. Spinach and kale are excellent choices that blend seamlessly while providing essential vitamins and minerals. The key I to start with a base of cooked rhubarb and then layer in your preferred greens, followed by fruits and a liquid base such as almond milk or coconut water. The result is a nutrient dense beverage that supports overall health, making it a perfect breakfast option or post workout refreshment.

For those who enjoy experimenting with flavors, consider adding spices such as ginger or cinnamon to your rhubarb smoothie. These spices not only enhance the drink's taste but also offer additional health benefits. Ginger can aid digestion, while cinnamon adds a hint of warmth and can help regulate blood sugar levels. You may also want to include protein sources like Greek yogurt or nut butter to create a more filling smoothie that can sustain your energy levels throughout the day, making it a great choice for busy mornings or an afternoon snack.

Finally, don't shy away from using rhubarb in creative smoothie recipes that cater to various dietary preferences. For gluten free options, you can easily substitute traditional ingredients with gluten free alternatives without sacrificing flavor. Additionally, consider incorporating seasonal produce to complement rhubarb, such as peaches in late summer or apples in the fall. By being adventurous with your ingredients, you can create smoothies that not only celebrate rhubarb's unique taste but also embrace the changing seasons and promote a healthy lifestyle.

Teas

Teas made with rhubarb offer a refreshing and unique way to enjoy this tart vegetable, transforming it into a delightful beverage that can be appreciated year round. Rhubarb's natural acidity and vibrant flavor lend themselves well to infusions, creating a drink that can be both soothing and invigorating. Whether served hot or cold, rhubarb tea can be easily integrated into your daily routine, providing an exciting twist on traditional herbal beverages. This subchapter will explore various methods of preparing rhubarb tea, its health benefits, and creative ways to enhance its flavor.

To prepare rhubarb tea, start by selecting fresh, vibrant stalks. The best rhubarb for tea is young and tender, showcasing a bright color, whether it be a deep red or a vibrant green. Begin by chopping the rhubarb into small pieces and simmering it in water for about 15 to 20 minutes. This process extracts the natural flavors and acidity of the rhubarb, resulting in a robust and aromatic brew. Strain the liquid to remove the solids, and you're left with a tangy tea that can be enjoyed as is or sweetened to taste.

Enhancing the flavor of rhubarb tea can be a delightful experiment.

Consider adding complementary ingredients such as ginger, mint, or lemon to create a more complex flavor profile. Ginger adds a warming spice that pairs beautifully with rhubarb's tartness, while fresh mint can introduce a refreshing note, perfect for iced versions. For a citrusy twist, a squeeze of lemon or a few slices of orange can brighten the tea and enhance its refreshing qualities. Sweeteners like honey or agave syrup can also be added, balancing out the acidity and making the tea more palatable for those who prefer a sweeter beverage.

The health benefits of rhubarb tea are worth noting as well. Rhubarb is low in calories but high in dietary fiber, which can aid digestion and promote a feeling of fullness. Additionally, it contains various vitamins and minerals, including vitamin K, vitamin C, and calcium. Drinking rhubarb tea can also provide antioxidants, which help combat oxidative stress in the body. Incorporating rhubarb tea into your diet may not only satisfy your thirst but also contribute positively to your overall health.

In conclusion, rhubarb tea is a versatile and healthful beverage that can be enjoyed in a variety of ways. Its tart flavor offers a refreshing departure from more conventional teas, and the possibilities for enhancement are nearly endless. Whether you prefer it hot or iced, sweetened or unsweetened, rhubarb tea can easily become a staple in your culinary repertoire. As you experiment with this delightful infusion, consider pairing it with other rhubarb based dishes to create a cohesive dining experience that celebrates the unique qualities of this underappreciated ingredient.

Chapter 4:

Rhubarb Preserves and Jams

Techniques for Canning Rhubarb

Canning rhubarb is an excellent way to preserve its unique tart flavor and vibrant color, allowing you to enjoy this versatile vegetable long after the growing season has ended. Whether you prefer it in sweet desserts, savory dishes, or refreshing beverages, mastering the art of canning rhubarb opens a world of culinary possibilities. The process is relatively straightforward, but it does require attention to detail and adherence to safe canning practices to ensure the end product is both delicious and safe for consumption.

Before you begin canning, it's crucial to select the right rhubarb. Look for firm stalks that are crisp and free from blemishes or soft spots. The color can vary from deep red to greenish; however, red stalks are often preferred for their color and sweetness. Once you have your rhubarb, wash it thoroughly and chop it into uniform pieces to ensure even cooking. For canning, it's advisable to use young rhubarb, as it is more tender and has a milder flavor.

The next step is to prepare your jars and lids. Sterilizing jars is essential to prevent bacteria from spoiling your preserves. You can do this by placing them in a boiling water bath for ten minutes. While the jars are sterilizing, prepare a rhubarb syrup or mixture.

A simple syrup can be made by combining equal parts sugar and water, which creates a sweet base that will complement the tartness of the rhubarb. Consider adding spices like cinnamon or ginger for an extra flavor kick.

Once your syrup is ready and your jars are sterilized, fill each jar with chopped rhubarb, leaving about half an inch of headspace. Pour the hot syrup over the rhubarb, ensuring that the pieces are fully submerged. Wipe the rims of the jars with a clean cloth to remove any residue, then seal them with sterilized lids. Process the jars in a boiling water bath for the recommended time, which can vary depending on your altitude and the size of the jars. This step is vital for creating a vacuum seal and ensuring the longevity of your canned rhubarb.

After processing, allow the jars to cool completely before checking the seals. A properly sealed jar will have a slight indentation in the center of the lid; if it pops back when pressed, it hasn't sealed correctly and should be refrigerated and consumed within a week. Canned rhubarb can be stored in a cool, dark place for up to a year, making it a delightful addition to your pantry. Whether you use it in desserts like pies and crumbles or in savory dishes, canned rhubarb offers versatility and a taste of summer year round.

Recipes for Rhubarb Preserves

Rhubarb preserves are a delightful way to capture the tart, refreshing flavor of this unique vegetable, transforming it into a sweet spread that can enhance various culinary experiences. These preserves are versatile and can be enjoyed on toast, as a filling for pastries, or even as a topping for savory dishes. Making rhubarb preserves is relatively simple, requiring minimal ingredients while allowing you to control the sweetness and texture to suit your preferences. In this subchapter, we will explore essential techniques and recipes to master the art of rhubarb preserves, ensuring that you can enjoy this vibrant ingredient throughout the year.

To begin, the basic recipe for rhubarb preserves involves just three key ingredients: rhubarb, sugar, and lemon juice. The first step is to prepare the rhubarb by washing and trimming the stalks before cutting them into small pieces. The natural tartness of rhubarb makes it essential to balance its flavor with sugar, which not only sweetens but also acts as a preservative. Adding lemon juice enhances the preserves' flavor and acidity, helping to maintain the vibrant color of the rhubarb while ensuring a longer shelf life. The mixture is then simmered gently on the stovetop, allowing the rhubarb to soften and release its juices, which will combine with the sugar to create a beautifully thickened preserve.

For those looking to experiment with flavors, various additions can elevate your rhubarb preserves to new heights. Consider incorporating spices like ginger or cinnamon for warmth, or zest from citrus fruits to add brightness. You can also blend rhubarb with other seasonal fruits such as strawberries or blueberries, creating a harmonious balance of sweetness and tang. These combinations not only enhance the flavor profile but also introduce a variety of colors and textures, making your preserves visually appealing. Each batch can be a creative endeavor, reflecting your personal taste and the seasonal produce available.

Canning is a crucial technique for preserving your rhubarb creations, ensuring they can be enjoyed long after the harvest season has passed. Sterilizing jars and lids is a vital step in the process, preventing spoilage and allowing your preserves to last for months. Once your rhubarb mixture has reached the desired consistency, ladle it into the hot, sterilized jars, leaving appropriate headspace for expansion while sealing them tightly. Process the jars in a water bath canner to create a vacuum seal, which will keep your preserves safe and flavorful. Properly canned rhubarb preserves can be stored in a cool, dark place, ready to be enjoyed during the off season.

Rhubarb preserves not only serve as a delicious spread but also provide numerous opportunities for culinary creativity. They can be used as a filling in pies and crumbles, lending their tartness to complement sweet pastries. For savory dishes, consider incorporating rhubarb preserves into glazes or sauces for meats, bringing a unique twist to your meals. Additionally, they can be stirred into yogurt or oatmeal for a quick breakfast or blended into cocktail and smoothies, showcasing rhubarb's versatility. By mastering the art of making rhubarb preserves, you can indulge in the delightful flavors of rhubarb year round, bringing a taste of spring to every season.

Creative Uses for Rhubarb Spreads

Rhubarb spreads, with their distinct tartness and vibrant color, offer a delightful twist to traditional condiments. While many may think of rhubarb solely as a filling for pies and crumbles, its versatility extends far beyond the dessert table. Incorporating rhubarb spreads into your culinary repertoire can elevate both savory and sweet dishes, making them more exciting and flavorful. This subchapter will explore various innovative ways to use rhubarb spreads that will appeal to anyone who enjoys food and is curious about the potential of this unique ingredient.

One of the most enjoyable ways to incorporate rhubarb spread is in breakfast dishes. Spread it over warm toast or scones for a refreshing alternative to traditional jams. The tartness of rhubarb complements creamy butters and cheeses beautifully. For a more decadent option, consider using rhubarb spread as a topping for pancakes or waffles, adding a drizzle of maple syrup or a dollop of whipped cream for a delightful brunch treat. This combination not only enhances the flavor profile of breakfast but also adds a burst of color to the plate, making your morning meal visually appealing.

Rhubarb spreads can also serve as a vibrant ingredient in savory dishes. Incorporating a spoonful into marinades for meats or as a glaze for roasted vegetables can introduce an unexpected depth of flavor. For instance, combining rhubarb spread with soy sauce, ginger, and garlic creates a unique marinade for grilled chicken or pork, lending a tangy sweetness that beautifully balances the savory elements. Additionally, stirring rhubarb spread into sauces or dressings can provide a refreshing twist to salads, particularly those featuring hearty greens and nuts.

For those looking to create memorable beverages, rhubarb spreads can be a fantastic addition to cocktails and smoothies. Mixing rhubarb spread with vodka, soda water, and a splash of lime creates a refreshing summer cocktail that captures the essence of the season. In smoothies, it pairs wonderfully with yogurt, bananas, and spinach, providing not only flavor but also a nutritious boost. The tartness of rhubarb can balance out sweeter fruits, making it an ideal ingredient for those seeking to create a well rounded drink that is both tasty and visually appealing.

Finally, rhubarb spreads can be a source of inspiration for creative desserts beyond the classic pie. Use rhubarb spread as a filling for gluten free cakes or as a layer in trifles, alongside creamy layers and fresh fruit. It can also serve as a base for rhubarb flavored frozen treats, such as popsicles or sorbets, which are perfect for warm days. By thinking outside the box, home cooks can explore the myriad of possibilities that rhubarb spreads offer, transforming everyday meals and snacks into extraordinary experiences.

In conclusion, rhubarb spreads are not just limited to breakfast or dessert; they are a versatile ingredient that can elevate a wide range of dishes. Whether used in sweet or savory applications, rhubarb spreads bring a unique flavor that can inspire creativity in the kitchen. By experimenting with this vibrant ingredient, anyone can discover new ways to enjoy rhubarb and enhance their culinary creations.

Chapter 5:

Gluten Free Rhubarb Recipes

Gluten Free Desserts with Rhubarb

Gluten free desserts have gained immense popularity as more people seek options that cater to dietary restrictions without compromising on flavor. Rhubarb, with its vibrant color and tart taste, serves as an excellent base for a variety of gluten free sweet treats. This unique vegetable pairs beautifully with natural sweeteners and gluten free flours, making it a versatile ingredient for those looking to create desserts that are both satisfying and suitable for gluten sensitive diets. One popular way to incorporate rhubarb into gluten free desserts is through pies and crumbles. A gluten free rhubarb pie can be made by using almond flour or a gluten free flour blend to create a flaky crust that complements the tartness of the rhubarb filling. Combining rhubarb with strawberries or other seasonal fruits not only enhances the flavor but also adds a touch of sweetness that balances the rhubarb's natural acidity. Crumbles, on the other hand, can feature a topping made from oats and gluten free flour mixed with butter, creating a delightful crunch that pairs perfectly with the soft, cooked rhubarb beneath.

Rhubarb cakes can also be a delightful addition to the gluten free dessert repertoire. By substituting traditional wheat flour with options like coconut flour or gluten free cake mixes, bakers can create moist and flavorful cakes that highlight the rhubarb's unique taste. Adding spices such as cinnamon or ginger can elevate the cake, making it a perfect treat for afternoon tea or a special occasion. Additionally, incorporating yogurt or applesauce can add moisture and richness, ensuring that the cake remains tender and satisfying.

For those who enjoy a chilled dessert, rhubarb can be transformed into a refreshing compote or a sorbet. A simple rhubarb compote can be made by simmering chopped rhubarb with a sweetener of choice, allowing the natural flavors to meld together. This compote can then be served over gluten free pancakes, yogurt, or simply enjoyed on its own. Alternatively, rhubarb sorbet offers a light and refreshing end to any meal. Blending cooked rhubarb with sugar and lemon juice before freezing creates a vibrant dessert that captures the essence of the season.

Incorporating rhubarb into gluten free desserts not only satisfies the sweet tooth but also highlights the health benefits associated with this unique vegetable. Rich in vitamins and antioxidants, rhubarb can be a nutritious addition to any dessert. By choosing natural sweeteners and gluten free ingredients, these desserts can easily fit into a health conscious lifestyle while providing the indulgence that dessert lovers crave. Experimenting with rhubarb in gluten free recipes opens up a world of culinary possibilities, inviting everyone to enjoy this versatile ingredient in delicious new ways.

Gluten Free Main Dishes Featuring Rhubarb

Rhubarb, often associated with sweet desserts, is a versatile ingredient that can elevate savory dishes, especially in gluten free cuisine. Incorporating rhubarb into main dishes opens up a world of flavor, combining its unique tartness with various proteins and vegetables. This subchapter explores how to transform rhubarb from a dessert staple into a central component of gluten free main courses. By utilizing the right cooking techniques and combinations, you can create dishes that are not only gluten free but also bursting with flavor and nutrition.

One popular way to feature rhubarb in a main dish is through savory sauces and glazes. A rhubarb reduction can serve as an excellent accompaniment for grilled meats or roasted vegetables. The tartness of the rhubarb balances beautifully with the richness of pork, chicken, or even Ash. Simply simmer chopped rhubarb with a splash of vinegar, honey, and aromatic herbs until it thickens into a luscious sauce. This can be drizzled over your protein of choice, providing a refreshing contrast that will surprise and delight diners.

Rhubarb also shines in grain free grain bowls, where it can serve as a bright pickled element. Quick pickling rhubarb adds tang and crunch, making it an ideal topping for bowls filled with quinoa, black rice, or roasted sweet potatoes. Combine the pickled rhubarb with other fresh vegetables, nuts, and a protein source like grilled tofu or seared chicken for a nutritious, gluten free meal. This approach not only highlights rhubarb's unique flavor but also enhances the dish's visual appeal with vibrant colors.

For a heartier option, consider incorporating rhubarb into savory casseroles or bakes. A gluten free shepherd's pie can take on an unexpected twist by adding rhubarb into the vegetable mixture. The cooking process softens the rhubarb and mellows its tartness, creating a complex flavor profile that complements the richness of the meat and mashed potatoes. This dish is not only comforting but also a creative way to introduce rhubarb into everyday meals, making it accessible to families looking to diversify their dinner menus.

Finally, rhubarb can play a pivotal role in international dishes that highlight its unique flavor while adhering to gluten free guidelines. In Indian cuisine, for example, rhubarb can be incorporated into curries, where its acidity adds depth to the spices. Similarly, Scandinavian dishes often feature rhubarb in savory applications, such as in a tangy sauce served with Ash or lamb. By exploring these global flavors, you can discover new ways to enjoy rhubarb while catering to gluten free diets, proving that this tart vegetable is more than just a sweet treat.

Snacks and Treats for Gluten Free Diets

Snacks and Treats for Gluten Free Diets

In the world of gluten free diets, finding satisfying snacks and treats can often feel like a daunting task. However, when incorporating rhubarb into the equation, a delightful array of options emerges that not only caters to gluten free needs but also tantalizes the taste buds. Rhubarb, with its vibrant color and tangy flavor, is an excellent ingredient to elevate snacks and desserts. Its versatility allows it to shine in both sweet and savory applications, making it a perfect companion for various gluten free recipes.

For those craving something sweet, rhubarb can be transformed into delicious gluten free treats like crumbles, pies, and muffins. A rhubarb crumble, for instance, can be made using almond flour and gluten free oats for the topping, creating a crunchy texture that complements the tartness of the rhubarb. Pairing this with a scoop of vanilla ice cream elevates it to a restaurant worthy dessert, perfect for any occasion. Additionally, gluten free rhubarb muffins provide a convenient and portable snack option, bursting with flavor and ideal for breakfast or an afternoon pick me up.

Savory snacks can also benefit from the unique flavor profile of rhubarb. Consider crafting a tangy rhubarb salsa, which can serve as a refreshing dip for gluten free tortilla chips. The combination of rhubarb with tomatoes, onions, and cilantro creates a zesty accompaniment that pairs beautifully ith grilled meats or fish. Another savory option is rhubarb infused cheese spreads, which can be served on gluten free crackers for a delightful appetizer that is sure to impress guests at any gathering.

For those who enjoy beverages, rhubarb can easily be transformed into refreshing drinks that are both gluten free and flavorful. A rhubarb and ginger iced tea or a rhubarb infused lemonade can provide a thirst quenching respite on warm days. Additionally, rhubarb works wonderfully in cocktails, where its tartness can balance the sweetness of spirits, making for intriguing gluten free mixology options. These beverages not only highlight rhubarb's versatility but also offer a unique twist to traditional drink recipes.

Incorporating rhubarb into gluten free snacks and treats not only provides delicious alternatives but also showcases the health benefits of this vibrant vegetable. Rich in vitamins and minerals, rhubarb adds a nutritional punch to recipes, making them enjoyable for both children and adults. Whether indulging in a sweet rhubarb cake or savoring tangy rhubarb salsa, these gluten free options allow everyone to enjoy the delightful flavors of rhubarb without compromising dietary needs. With creativity and a focus on quality ingredients, the world of gluten free snacking can be both satisfying and flavorful.

Chapter 6:

Rhubarb and Seasonal Produce Pairings

Spring Pairings: Rhubarb with Strawberries

Spring is a season that heralds fresh beginnings, and few combinations embody this renewal as beautifully as rhubarb and strawberries. This dynamic duo, with rhubarb's tartness and strawberries' sweetness, not only delights the palate but also offers a vibrant palette of colors and textures that brighten any dish. As the warmer months approach, these two ingredients become the stars of the kitchen, inspiring a variety of recipes that celebrate their unique flavors. From classic desserts to innovative savory dishes, rhubarb and strawberries are a match made in culinary heaven.

In the realm of desserts, the pairing of rhubarb and strawberries is timeless. Rhubarb's natural acidity complements the sweetness of ripe strawberries, creating an exquisite balance that shines in pies, crumbles, and cakes. A traditional strawberry rhubarb pie, for instance, showcases this harmony beautifully, with a flaky crust enveloping a bubbling filling that bursts with summer flavors. For those looking to explore gluten free options, a gluten free strawberry rhubarb crumble made with almond flour or oats can provide the same satisfying experience without the gluten. The combination can also be transformed into cakes or tarts, where the tangy flavor of rhubarb cuts through the sweetness, making these desserts refreshing and delightful.

Savory dishes can also benefit from the lively contrast of rhubarb and strawberries. While many associate rhubarb primarily with sweet applications, its acidity can enhance main courses and sides. Imagine a grilled chicken dish glazed with a rhubarb strawberry reduction, where the tartness of rhubarb adds depth to the natural sweetness of strawberries, creating a bright, flavorful sauce. Additionally, incorporating rhubarb into salads, perhaps paired with spinach, toasted nuts, and a light vinaigrette, can provide a surprising twist that elevates your dining experience. This versatility encourages creativity in the kitchen as cooks explore the less conventional uses of rhubarb.

The refreshing qualities of rhubarb and strawberries also lend themselves well to beverages. Their bright flavors can transform simple drinks into seasonal delights. A rhubarb strawberry smoothie, for example, not only provides a burst of flavor but also packs a nutritional punch. For those looking to indulge, crafting a rhubarb strawberry cocktail can be a show stopping addition to any spring gathering. The tartness of rhubarb contrasts beautifully with spirits and mixers, offering a unique and refreshing drink option that is sure to impress guests.

Lastly, preserving the flavors of spring can be achieved through making jams and preserves that highlight the rhubarb strawberry combination. Canning these ingredients allows you to enjoy the taste of spring long after the season has passed. The process of making preserves is not only rewarding but also a wonderful way to capture the essence of this dynamic pairing. Whether slathered on toast or used as a filling for pastries, rhubarb strawberry preserves bring a taste of spring to your table year round. By exploring the various ways to utilize rhubarb and strawberries together, you can create a repertoire of dishes that celebrate the best of both ingredients, enhancing your culinary journey with each recipe.

Summer Pairings: Rhubarb with Berries

Summer is the perfect season to celebrate the vibrant flavors of fresh produce, and when it comes to seasonal pairings, rhubarb and berries create a delightful combination that is hard to resist. Rhubarb, with its tart profile, complements the sweetness of various berries, making them a natural duo in both desserts and savory dishes. This subchapter will explore how to harness the unique characteristics of rhubarb alongside strawberries, blueberries, raspberries, and blackberries, allowing cooks of all skill levels to create dishes that burst with flavor and showcase the best of summer's bounty.

The magic of this pairing is most evident in desserts. Classic rhubarb and berry pies are a staple in many homes during the warmer months. The tartness of the rhubarb balances the sweetness of the berries, creating a harmonious filling that is perfect between flaky layers of crust. For an easy twist, consider a rhubarb and berry crumble, where the sweet, buttery topping adds a delightful crunch to the tender fruit beneath. Not only are these desserts satisfying, but they also highlight the health benefits of rhubarb and berries, which are rich in antioxidants and vitamins, making them a guilt free indulgence.

Savory dishes can also benefit from the addition of rhubarb and berries. Incorporating them into salads or as a tangy sauce can elevate the flavor profile of meats, particularly chicken or pork. A rhubarb berry compote can serve as a refreshing condiment, providing a sweet and tangy contrast that enhances the dish without overpowering it. This approach not only showcases the versatility of rhubarb but also encourages adventurous home cooks to experiment with their flavor combinations, transforming traditional recipes into something uniquely their own.

For those interested in beverages, rhubarb's tartness lends itself beautifully to summer drinks. A rhubarb and berry smoothie can be a refreshing way to start the day, while cocktails featuring these ingredients can be a perfect addition to any summer gathering. Think of a rhubarb berry fizz or a punch that combines the brightness of both fruits with sparkling water or a splash of gin. These drinks not only quench thirst but also provide an opportunity to enjoy the flavors of summer in a new and exciting way.

Finally, preserving the flavors of summer can be accomplished through canning rhubarb and berry jams or sauces. These preserves allow you to enjoy the essence of summer even during the colder months. The process of making jam is straightforward and rewarding, and the resulting spreads can be used in a variety of ways from topping for toast to filling for gluten free pastries. By mastering these techniques, anyone can savor the delightful summer pairing of rhubarb and berries well beyond the season, ensuring that this vibrant flavor combination remains a staple in their culinary repertoire.

Fall and Winter Pairings: Rhubarb with Apples and Squash

In the world of culinary pairings, few combinations evoke the comforting essence of fall and winter quite like rhubarb with apples and squash. These ingredients not only celebrate the season's bounty but also create a delightful harmony of flavors and textures. Rhubarb, with its tartness, brings a unique twist to traditional dishes, enhancing the sweetness of apples and the earthy richness of squash. This chapter delves into how to effectively combine these ingredients in various recipes, ensuring that you can enjoy the best of what each season has to offer.

To start with the pairing of rhubarb and apples, consider the classic charm of a rhubarb apple pie. The tartness of rhubarb complements the natural sweetness of apples, resulting in a filling that strikes a perfect balance. When preparing this dish, opt for a mix of tart and sweet apple varieties, such as Granny Smith and Honey crisp, to deepen the flavor profile. Adding a sprinkle of cinnamon and nutmeg can further enhance the warmth of the pie, making it a comforting treat ideal for chilly evenings. This pairing is not limited to desserts; a savory rhubarb apple chutney can accompany roasted meats, providing a tangy contrast that elevates the dish.

Squash, particularly varieties like butternut and acorn, offers a different yet equally rewarding pairing with rhubarb. The creamy texture and sweetness of roasted squash create a beautiful backdrop for rhubarb's tartness. A simple dish of roasted squash drizzled with a rhubarb vinaigrette can serve as a stunning salad or side dish. To make the vinaigrette, simmer rhubarb with honey, vinegar, and mustard until it breaks down into a sauce. This dressing not only adds flavor but also a vibrant color, making your plate visually appealing. The combination is both nutritious and satisfying, showcasing how rhubarb can enhance vegetable centric dishes.

Exploring rhubarb in beverages also opens up exciting possibilities, especially paired with apples and squash. A warming rhubarb apple cider can be an excellent choice for gatherings during the fall and winter months. Simply combine fresh apple cider with rhubarb syrup and spices like clove and cinnamon, then heat gently. This drink not only warms you from the inside out but also introduces guests to the unexpected yet delightful flavor of rhubarb. Alternatively, consider a refreshing rhubarb squash smoothie, blending roasted squash with rhubarb juice for a nutrient packed drink that can serve as a quick breakfast or a post workout rejuvenation.

Finally, when considering storage and preservation, rhubarb pairs beautifully with these seasonal ingredients in preserves and jams.

Making a rhubarb apple preserve can be an excellent way to capture the essence of fall in a jar. The process involves cooking down rhubarb and apples with sugar and lemon juice until it reaches a spreadable consistency. This preserve can serve multiple purposes, from a delightful addition to breakfast toast to a topping for desserts or even as a glaze for meats. The versatility of rhubarb shines through once more, as it melds seamlessly with other ingredients, adding a touch of tartness to sweet and savory applications alike.

In conclusion, the fall and winter pairings of rhubarb with apples and squash not only highlight the seasonal characteristics of these ingredients but also invite creativity in the kitchen. Whether in desserts, savory dishes, drinks, or preserves, these combinations promise to bring warmth and flavor to your table. Embrace the opportunity to experiment with these pairings, and you'll discover new favorites that celebrate the unique qualities of rhubarb throughout the colder months.

Chapter 7:

Rhubarb for Kids

Fun and Easy Rhubarb Desserts

Fun and Easy Rhubarb Desserts

Rhubarb is a unique ingredient that can elevate dessert recipes with its vibrant color and tart flavor. In this section, we will explore fun and easy rhubarb desserts that anyone can master, whether you're a seasoned baker or just starting your culinary journey. With its versatility, rhubarb can be transformed into a variety of sweet treats, from classic pies and crumbles to modern cakes and tarts. These recipes not only highlight the distinct taste of rhubarb but also engage the creativity of home cooks, making them perfect for family gatherings or casual weeknight dinners.

One of the simplest and most recognizable rhubarb desserts is the classic rhubarb pie. This dish combines the tartness of rhubarb with a sweet, flaky crust and is often enhanced with complementary flavors such as strawberries or ginger. To make the filling, simply mix chopped rhubarb with sugar, a touch of cornstarch for thickening, and your chosen spices. Pour this mixture into a prepared pie crust, top with another layer or a lattice design, and bake until bubbly and golden brown. The result is a comforting dessert that showcases the natural flavors of rhubarb while inviting everyone to indulge in a slice.

For those who prefer a more casual dessert, rhubarb crumble is an excellent choice. This dish allows for easy preparation and customization. Start with a base of rhubarb mixed with sugar and a little lemon juice for brightness. Top it off with a crumbly mixture of oats, flour, butter, and brown sugar, then bake until the topping is golden and the rhubarb is tender. This dessert is perfect served warm with a scoop of vanilla ice cream or a dollop of whipped cream, making it a crowd pleaser at any gathering. Plus, it can be made gluten free by substituting the flour with almond flour or gluten free oats.

Cakes featuring rhubarb are another delightful option that can impress guests with minimal effort. A rhubarb upside down cake offers a stunning presentation and a burst of flavor in every bite. Simply arrange rhubarb slices in a cake pan, pour over a buttery cake batter, and bake. When flipped, the cake reveals a beautiful layer of caramelized rhubarb that is both visually appealing and delicious. For a lighter option, consider making rhubarb muffins or cupcakes, where the tartness of rhubarb balances the sweetness of the batter, creating a tasty treat that pairs well with morning coffee or afternoon tea.

Finally, don't overlook the potential for rhubarb in no bake desserts, which can be especially appealing during the warmer months. A rhubarb cheesecake or parfait can be made by incorporating a rhubarb compote, which is simply rhubarb cooked down with sugar until it becomes a thick syrup. Layer this compote with cream cheese or yogurt and your choice of graham cracker or cookie crumbs for a refreshing dessert that requires no oven. Such recipes not only save time but also allow for a fun and interactive experience, particularly when involving kids in the kitchen.

In conclusion, rhubarb desserts offer a delightful way to experiment with this tart vegetable in sweet applications. From pies and crumbles to cakes and no bake treats, there is a wide range of options that cater to different tastes and preferences. These fun and easy recipes encourage creativity in the kitchen while celebrating the unique flavor of rhubarb, making them perfect for anyone who loves food and wants to explore this versatile ingredient. Whether you're baking for family, friends, or simply treating yourself, these rhubarb desserts are sure to impress and satisfy.

Kid Friendly Savory Dishes

Kid friendly savory dishes can be an exciting way to introduce children to the unique flavor of rhubarb while ensuring that meals appeal to their taste buds. Rhubarb, often associated with desserts, can also shine in savory applications, lending its tartness to enhance flavors in various dishes. When preparing meals for children, it's essential to balance flavors and textures, ensuring that the dishes are not only nutritious but also visually appealing and fun to eat.

One delightful option is rhubarb infused chicken stir fry. By combining tender chicken pieces with vibrant vegetables such as bell peppers and snap peas, you can create a colorful dish. The addition of rhubarb, sliced thin and sautéed briefly, adds a zesty punch that complements the savory elements. To make this dish even more appealing to kids, serve it over a bed of fluffy rice or noodles, allowing the tangy rhubarb sauce to coat each bite. This dish not only introduces children to new flavors but also encourages them to enjoy a variety of vegetables.

Another creative savory dish is rhubarb quesadillas. By mixing finely chopped rhubarb with cheese and your choice of protein such as beans or chicken you can create a filling that is both delicious and nutritious. The quesadillas can be grilled until golden and crispy, making them an irresistible option for children. Pairing these quesadillas with a simple avocado dip or salsa adds extra flavor and nutrition, while the fun of dipping can make mealtime more engaging for young eaters. For a comforting option, consider making a rhubarb and vegetable soup.

This vibrant soup, enriched with carrots, potatoes, and celery, relies on rhubarb to provide a natural tanginess that balances the sweetness of the vegetables. Pureeing the soup until smooth can create a delightful texture that appeals to children, who may be more willing to try new flavors if they are presented in a familiar form. Topped with a dollop of yogurt or a sprinkle of cheese, this soup becomes both eye catching and inviting.

Finally, rhubarb can be incorporated into savory muffins or scones, which are perfect for snacking or breakfast. By adding finely chopped rhubarb along with cheese and herbs, these baked goods can offer a delightful twist on traditional recipes. Kids love finger foods, and these savory treats can be made in mini sizes, making them easy to grab for busy mornings or lunchboxes. Such recipes not only provide a way to enjoy the goodness of rhubarb but also encourage children to embrace a variety of flavors and ingredients in their diet.

Incorporating rhubarb into kid friendly savory dishes not only broadens culinary experiences for children but also enhances their appreciation for diverse flavors. These creative approaches to rhubarb can foster a love for cooking and eating, encouraging young ones to explore the world of flavors beyond the usual sweet treats. By making savory rhubarb dishes fun, colorful, and easy to prepare, families can enjoy quality time together in the kitchen while nourishing their bodies with healthy ingredients.

Engaging Kids in Rhubarb Cooking

Engaging kids in rhubarb cooking can be a delightful way to introduce them to the joys of culinary creativity while fostering a love for healthy eating. Rhubarb, with its vibrant color and unique tart flavor, presents an excellent opportunity for children to explore the kitchen. By involving kids in the cooking process, they can learn valuable skills, and have fun experimenting with this versatile ingredient. This subchapter will provide enjoyable and easy rhubarb recipes tailored for young chefs, emphasizing the importance of hands on learning in the kitchen.

One of the best ways to start engaging kids with rhubarb is by involving them in simple, hands on recipes. Classic rhubarb crisps or crumbles are perfect introductory dishes. Children can help wash and chop the rhubarb, mix it with sweeteners, and sprinkle the crumbly topping. Not only does this teach them basic cooking techniques, but it also allows them to see how the tartness of rhubarb can be balanced with sugar and other ingredients. Additionally, they can take pride in presenting a dish they helped create, reinforcing the idea that cooking can be both fun and rewarding.

Incorporating rhubarb into beverages can also engage children's interest I cooking. Recipes for rhubarb smoothies or mock tails can be particularly appealing. Kids can take charge of blending the ingredients, experimenting with flavors by adding fruits like strawberries or bananas, and learning about the different textures that result from blending. Making drinks is an exciting and interactive way for them to learn about the ingredient's versatility while enjoying a refreshing treat. These activities can also serve as an opportunity to discuss the health benefits of rhubarb, such as its high fiber content and various vitamins.

Exploring rhubarb desserts offers another avenue for engaging kids, particularly through baking. Making a rhubarb pie or cake can be a fulfilling project. Children can participate in rolling out the dough, filling the pie, or decorating the cake. This experience not only teaches them the fundamentals of baking but also encourages creativity as they choose how to decorate their creations. Moreover, by preparing dishes that are visually appealing, kids are more likely to be excited about trying new flavors, including the unique tang of rhubarb.

Finally, encouraging kids to pair rhubarb with seasonal fruits and vegetables can stimulate their interest in gardening and understanding where food comes from. Organizing a family outing to a local farmer's market or planting a small rhubarb patch can create a deeper connection to the ingredient. Together, families can experiment with recipes that combine rhubarb with strawberries, apples, or even savory vegetables like carrots. This not only teaches kids about seasonal eating but also helps them appreciate the flavors and nutritional benefits of fresh produce. Engaging kids n rhubarb cooking can nurture their culinary skills, foster a love for healthy eating, and create lasting family memories in the kitchen.

Chapter 8:

Rhubarb in International Cuisine

Indian Rhubarb Dishes

Indian cuisine offers a vibrant array of flavors, and incorporating rhubarb into traditional Indian dishes adds an intriguing twist that enhances both taste and texture. Indian rhubarb dishes often balance the vegetable's tartness with spices and sweetness, creating a unique fusion that appeals to adventurous palates. Rhubarb can be used in various forms, from curries to chutneys, allowing cooks to experiment with its bold flavor profile while adhering to traditional cooking methods.

One delightful way to incorporate rhubarb is through a tangy rhubarb curry. This dish typically features rhubarb cooked down with a medley of spices, including cumin, coriander, and turmeric, along with onions and tomatoes. The resulting mixture blends the sharpness of the rhubarb with the warmth of the spices, creating a complex and satisfying dish. When served alongside rice or flatbreads, this curry transforms a simple meal into a vibrant experience, showcasing rhubarb as a versatile ingredient in Indian cuisine.

Rhubarb can also shine in Indian chutneys, which serve as flavorful accompaniments to many meals. A rhubarb and mint chutney, for example, combines the tartness of rhubarb with fresh mint, green chilies, and a touch of jiggery or sugar for sweetness. This chutney can be served alongside grilled meats, samosas, or even as a flavorful spread on sandwiches. The brightness of the chutney enhances the overall dining experience, making it a refreshing counterpoint to richer dishes.

For those seeking a sweet finish, rhubarb can be incorporated into traditional Indian desserts, such as kheer or halva. Rhubarb kheer, made with rice, milk, and sugar, can be elevated by adding cooked rhubarb to the mix, infusing the creamy dessert with a subtle tang. Similarly, rhubarb halva, prepared with semolina and sweetened with sugar, can include rhubarb for an unexpected yet delightful twist. These desserts not only highlight the versatility of rhubarb but also demonstrate how it can be embraced within the framework of classic Indian sweets.

In summary, exploring Indian rhubarb dishes allows cooks to experience the delightful interplay of flavors that rhubarb can bring to traditional recipes. Whether in savory curries, zesty chutneys, or sweet desserts, rhubarb's tartness complements the spices and ingredients inherent in Indian cuisine, resulting in dishes that are both innovative and deeply satisfying. Embracing rhubarb in this culinary context opens up new avenues for creativity and enjoyment, making it an exciting ingredient for anyone who loves food and wishes to experiment with flavors from around the world.

Scandinavian Rhubarb Recipes

Scandinavian cuisine has long embraced the unique tartness of rhubarb, transforming it into a beloved ingredient in both sweet and savory dishes. This subchapter delves into traditional and contemporary Scandinavian rhubarb recipes that highlight its versatility, making it a delightful addition to any meal. Rhubarb's vibrant flavor pairs beautifully with the region's seasonal produce, creating dishes that reflect the essence of Scandinavian cooking.

One of the most cherished ways to enjoy rhubarb in Scandinavian kitchens is through desserts like pies, crumbles, and cakes. Rhubarb pie, often combined with strawberries or custard, showcases the fruit's tangy profile against a buttery crust, offering a balance of flavors. Crumbles, on the other hand, are a quick and comforting option, allowing for a crunchy oat topping that complements the tender rhubarb beneath. For those seeking a twist on traditional cakes, a rhubarb upside down cake can be a showstopper, presenting a stunning visual while delivering a sweet and sour taste experience.

Beyond desserts, rhubarb can also shine in savory dishes, adding a refreshing acidity that cuts through rich flavors. Scandinavian recipes often incorporate rhubarb into hearty main courses or side dishes. For instance, rhubarb can be braised with pork or chicken, imparting a unique depth to the dish. Additionally, rhubarb chutneys serve as a delicious condiment alongside grilled meats or cheese platters, offering an unexpected yet delightful flavor that enhances the overall dining experience.

Beverages crafted with rhubarb are another exciting aspect of Scandinavian culinary traditions. Rhubarb juice, often sweetened and carbonated, can be served as a refreshing drink during the warmer months. For a more adult twist, rhubarb cocktails featuring gin or vodka bring out the tartness in a sophisticated manner. Smoothies that blend rhubarb with yogurt and seasonal fruits provide a nutritious option for breakfast or a light snack, while herbal teas infused with rhubarb can offer a soothing end to the day.

Lastly, Scandinavian rhubarb recipes often emphasize preservation techniques, allowing this seasonal delight to be enjoyed year round. Making rhubarb preserves or jams is a popular way to capture its flavor, perfect for spreading on toast or incorporating into pastries. For those following gluten free diets,

Scandinavian recipes can be easily adapted by using gluten free flours in baked goods. This versatility ensures that everyone can enjoy the delightful taste of rhubarb while embracing the health benefits this vibrant vegetable offers, such as its high fiber content and low calorie profile. Through these recipes, Scandinavian rhubarb shines as an ingredient that brings families together around the table.

Other Global Rhubarb Inspirations

In exploring the diverse culinary applications of rhubarb, it is essential to consider the global inspirations that highlight this unique ingredient's versatility. Rhubarb, often perceived primarily as a sweet filling for pies and desserts, has found its way into a multitude of international cuisines, showcasing its ability to enhance both savory and sweet dishes. From tangy chutneys in India to refreshing drinks in Scandinavia, rhubarb's tart flavor profile brings an exciting twist to various global recipes that appeal to food lovers around the world.

One notable example of rhubarb's incorporation into international cuisine is found in the traditional Indian chutney, which combines rhubarb with spices and sugar to create a vibrant condiment. This chutney not only serves as a delightful accompaniment to curries and flatbreads but also introduces a unique tartness that balances the rich flavors typically found in Indian dishes. The fusion of rhubarb with spices like cumin and coriander offers a fresh take on a beloved staple, proving that this vegetable can transcend its conventional use in desserts and become a key player in savory applications.

In Scandinavian countries, rhubarb is often celebrated in the springtime, here it is used in a variety of refreshing beverages. A popular choice is rhubarb juice, which combines the tartness of the stalks with sweeteners and sometimes hints of ginger or mint. This drink not only quenches thirst but also encapsulates the essence of the season, making it a favorite among locals. Additionally, rhubarb is frequently featured in traditional dishes such as stews and salads, where it complements other seasonal produce, enhancing both flavor and nutrition.

The versatility of rhubarb extends to its role in desserts across different cultures, where it is often paired with ingredients unique to those regions. In Scandinavian baking, for instance, rhubarb is frequently used in crumbles and pies, often combined with berries that grow abundantly in the area. These desserts celebrate the natural sweetness of the fruits while allowing the rhubarb's tartness to shine through. In contrast, Middle Eastern desserts often incorporate rhubarb in syrups and compotes, which are drizzled over pastries, providing a delightful contrast to the rich flavors of the sweets.

As we continue to explore the myriad ways to enjoy rhubarb, it becomes clear that its global inspirations offer a wealth of culinary possibilities. Whether it's through savory dishes that incorporate spices or refreshing beverages that highlight its tartness, rhubarb proves to be a versatile ingredient that can adapt to various palates and preferences. For those interested in expanding their rhubarb repertoire, these international recipes not only provide exciting new flavors but also celebrate the cultural significance of this remarkable vegetable in kitchens around the world.

Chapter 9:

Rhubarb Health Benefits

Nutritional Profile of Rhubarb

Rhubarb is a unique and versatile vegetable often mistaken for fruit, celebrated for its tart flavor and vibrant color. While it may not be the first vegetable that comes to mind when considering health benefits, rhubarb boasts a remarkable nutritional profile that can complement a variety of dishes, from desserts to savory meals. This subchapter will delve into the nutritional components of rhubarb, highlighting its vitamins, minerals, and overall health benefits.

At the heart of rhubarb's nutritional appeal is its impressive low calorie count. A cup of raw rhubarb, which weighs approximately 120 grams, contains only about 26 calories. This makes it an excellent choice for those looking to maintain or lose weight without sacrificing flavor. In addition to being low in calories, rhubarb is also high in dietary fiber, which aids in digestion and promotes a feeling of fullness. This fiber content can be especially beneficial in gluten free recipes, where rhubarb can provide bulk and texture.

Rhubarb is rich in essential vitamins and minerals, particularly vitamin K, which plays a crucial role in bone health and blood coagulation. A single serving of rhubarb can provide a significant portion of the recommended daily intake of this vital nutrient. Additionally, rhubarb contains vitamin C, an antioxidant that supports the immune system and skin health. The presence of potassium, manganese, and calcium further enhances its nutritional value, making it a worthy addition to a balanced diet.

The health benefits of rhubarb extend beyond its vitamin and mineral content. The vegetable is known for its potential anti inflammatory properties, which can help alleviate symptoms of various conditions. Moreover, research indicates that the antioxidants found in rhubarb may contribute to reducing oxidative stress in the body, promoting overall wellness. For those interested in health conscious recipes, incorporating rhubarb into smoothies, salads, or even savory dishes can enhance both taste and nutritional value.

In summary, rhubarb is not just a flavorful ingredient for pies and crumbles; it is a nutrient dense vegetable that can play a significant role in a healthy diet. Its low calorie and high fiber content, combined with a wealth of vitamins and minerals, make it an excellent choice for various culinary applications. Whether you are experimenting with rhubarb in desserts, savory dishes, or beverages, understanding its nutritional profile can inspire you to incorporate this unique vegetable into your cooking repertoire, benefiting both your palate and your health.

Cooking with Health in Mind

Cooking with health in mind is an essential aspect of enjoying food, and rhubarb offers a unique opportunity to incorporate nutritious ingredients into a variety of dishes. Known for its vibrant color and tart flavor, rhubarb is not only a versatile ingredient in the kitchen but also boasts several health benefits. This subchapter will explore how to elevate your culinary creations using rhubarb while focusing on nutritional value, making it a delightful addition to your meals.

Rhubarb is low in calories and high in dietary fiber, making it an excellent ingredient for those looking to maintain a healthy lifestyle. It contains essential vitamins and minerals, including vitamin K, vitamin C, and calcium, which contribute to overall well being. When crafting your rhubarb recipes, consider pairing it with other seasonal produce to enhance both flavor and nutritional content. For instance, combining rhubarb with strawberries not only creates a delightful dessert but also adds a boost of antioxidants and vitamins, making your dish both delicious and health conscious.

Incorporating rhubarb into savory dishes is another way to enjoy its health benefits. Rhubarb's tartness can complement a variety of proteins and vegetables. For example, a rhubarb infused sauce can elevate grilled meats or roasted vegetables, adding a unique twist while keeping the dish light. By experimenting with savory rhubarb recipes, you can create meals that are both satisfying and packed with nutrients, making healthy eating enjoyable for the whole family.

Drinks can also be a fantastic way to incorporate rhubarb into your diet. Rhubarb cocktails, smoothies, and teas not only celebrate its distinctive flavor but can also be made with health in mind. When crafting these beverages, opt for natural sweeteners or use fruits that enhance the drink's nutritional profile. Rhubarb smoothies, for instance, can be paired with spinach or kale for an extra dose of vitamins and minerals, creating a refreshing treat that nourishes the body.

Lastly, preserving rhubarb through jams and spreads can be a delightful way to enjoy its flavor year round while keeping health in focus. Utilizing low sugar techniques or incorporating other fruits can enhance the nutritional value of your preserves. When canning rhubarb, consider using gluten free methods to cater to various dietary needs, ensuring everyone can enjoy your homemade creations. Cooking with health in mind not only enriches your meals but also fosters a greater appreciation for the beautiful, versatile rhubarb plant.

Incorporating Rhubarb into a Balanced Diet

Incorporating rhubarb into a balanced diet can enhance both flavor and nutrition, making it a versatile ingredient for various culinary applications. This tart vegetable, often mistaken for a fruit, packs a punch in terms of taste and health benefits. Rich in vitamins C and K, fiber, and antioxidants, rhubarb can play a significant role in promoting overall wellness. By understanding how to integrate rhubarb into your meals, you can enjoy its unique flavor while reaping its nutritional rewards.

One of the most popular ways to enjoy rhubarb is through desserts such as pies, crumbles, and cakes. These sweet treats highlight the natural tartness of rhubarb, which balances well with sugars and other fruits. For those who love baking, consider incorporating rhubarb into classic recipes like strawberry rhubarb pie or rhubarb crumble, where its acidity enhances the sweetness of other ingredients. Additionally, experimenting with gluten free alternatives can make these beloved desserts accessible to a wider audience, ensuring that everyone can enjoy the delightful combination of flavors.

Rhubarb isn't just for sweets; it can also add a unique twist to savory dishes. Incorporating rhubarb into main courses and sides can elevate your meals and introduce exciting flavor profiles. For instance, using rhubarb in sauces for meats, such as pork or chicken, can create a refreshing contrast that balances richness with its acidity. Likewise, adding rhubarb to stir fries or salads can provide a crunchy texture and a zesty kick, making your meals more interesting and nutritious.

For those looking to explore refreshing beverages, rhubarb can be a fantastic ingredient in cocktails, smoothies, and teas. Its tartness pairs well with various flavors, making it an excellent choice for vibrant drinks. Consider crafting a rhubarb infused spritzer or blending it into a smoothie with seasonal fruits for a refreshing treat. These beverages not only satisfy your thirst but also offer a unique way to enjoy the health benefits of rhubarb while impressing friends and family with creative concoctions.

Finally, preserving rhubarb through jams and spreads is an excellent method to enjoy its flavor year round. Using canning techniques, you can create delicious rhubarb preserves that serve as a delightful topping for toast or desserts. Additionally, combining rhubarb with other seasonal produce can result in unique flavor profiles and nutritious spreads. Whether it's pairing rhubarb with strawberries, apples, or even spices, the possibilities are endless. Incorporating rhubarb into your balanced diet can be both enjoyable and healthful, allowing you to savor its distinctive taste while keeping your meals exciting and diverse.

Chapter 10:

Conclusion

Embracing Rhubarb in Everyday Cooking

Embracing rhubarb in everyday cooking opens a world of culinary possibilities that can elevate both simple meals and elaborate dishes. Renowned for its vibrant color and unique tart flavor, rhubarb is a versatile ingredient that can be incorporated into various recipes, ranging from desserts to savory main courses. By understanding how to use rhubarb effectively, home cooks can introduce this underappreciated vegetable into their daily repertoire, transforming ordinary dishes into extraordinary experiences.

When it comes to desserts, rhubarb shines as a star ingredient, particularly in pies, crumbles, and cakes. The tartness of rhubarb balances beautifully with the sweetness of sugar, making it an ideal candidate for classic desserts. A traditional rhubarb pie, for instance, combines fresh rhubarb with sugar and hint of cinnamon, all encased in a flaky crust. Crumbles and cakes can also highlight rhubarb's tangy essence, with recipes that incorporate it into the batter or as a topping. Exploring variations, such as gluten free options, ensures that everyone can enjoy these delectable treats without compromising on flavor.

Savory dishes featuring rhubarb are often overlooked but can introduce an exciting twist to everyday meals. Its acidity can enhance flavors in main courses and side dishes, making it a perfect companion for meats like pork or chicken. For instance, a rhubarb chutney can serve as a zesty condiment, while roasted rhubarb can add a surprising element to salads or grain bowls. Pairing rhubarb with seasonal produce not only showcases its versatility but also promotes a farm to table approach that celebrates the best of what each season has to offer.

Beverages are another delightful way to embrace rhubarb's unique flavor. Rhubarb can be transformed into refreshing cocktails, smoothies, and teas that are perfect for any occasion. A rhubarb infused gin and tonic or a smoothie blending rhubarb with strawberries and yogurt makes for a vibrant, health conscious choice. Moreover, crafting homemade rhubarb syrups can enhance drinks while allowing for creative experimentation. These beverages not only highlight rhubarb's tartness but also offer a refreshing alternative to traditional drink options.

Finally, preserving rhubarb through jams and spreads allows for enjoyment beyond the growing season. Canning techniques can be employed to create delightful rhubarb preserves, making it easy to enjoy the vegetable long after harvest. These can be used as toppings for breakfast items or as a sweet element in savory dishes. The health benefits of rhubarb, including its high fiber content and low calorie count, can also be emphasized in recipes hat focus on wellness. By integrating rhubarb into various aspects of daily cooking, individuals can cultivate a deeper appreciation for this unique ingredient, turning it into a staple in their culinary adventures.

Final Thoughts on Rhubarb Creativity

In the culinary world, rhubarb stands out as a unique ingredient that offers both inspiration and versatility. As we conclude our exploration of this remarkable plant in "The Rhubarb Cookbook: Mastering Cooking Techniques and Storage Tips," it is essential to recognize the creativity it can spark in both novice and seasoned cooks. Whether you're baking delightful desserts or crafting savory dishes, rhubarb's tartness invites a playful approach to flavor combinations, encouraging experimentation and innovation in the kitchen.

Rhubarb's potential extends far beyond traditional desserts like pies and crumbles. Its vibrant acidity can elevate main courses and side dishes, adding a surprising twist to familiar recipes. From savory rhubarb chutneys that complement grilled meats to rhubarb infused sauces that enhance seasonal vegetables, this ingredient can transform an ordinary meal into an extraordinary culinary experience. Encouraging readers to think outside the box may lead to discovering unique pairings with seasonal produce, creating dishes that celebrate the flavors of each season.

Moreover, rhubarb's versatility shines through in beverages and preserves. From refreshing rhubarb cocktails to soothing teas, the plant's tartness can be harnessed to create drinks that tantalize the taste buds. Additionally, techniques for canning rhubarb into jams and preserves provide a wonderful way to enjoy its flavor year round. These creations not only enhance the dining experience but also offer opportunities for sharing homemade gifts, making them a delightful addition to any occasion.

For those with dietary restrictions, rhubarb can easily fit into gluten free recipes, offering a range of options that cater to diverse needs. Its health benefits are also noteworthy, as it is low in calories and rich in antioxidants, making it a nutritious choice for anyone looking to enhance their diet. By incorporating rhubarb into health focused recipes, we can promote wellness without sacrificing flavor, proving that indulgence and nutrition can coexist harmoniously.

In conclusion, the journey through the world of rhubarb is an invitation to unleash creativity in the kitchen. As we experiment with its myriad applications from desserts and savory dishes to beverages and preserves we find that rhubarb is more than just a seasonal ingredient; it is a catalyst for culinary exploration. Encourage yourself and your loved ones to embrace this vibrant plant, allowing it to inspire new dishes and unforgettable flavor experiences. Let rhubarb remind us that cooking is not only about nourishment but also about joy, creativity, and the shared love of food.

Encouragement for Home Cooks

Home cooking is an art form, and when it comes to incorporating rhubarb into your culinary repertoire, the possibilities are as vast as your creativity allows. Whether you are an experienced cook or just starting your kitchen journey, embracing rhubarb can elevate your dishes from ordinary to extraordinary. This versatile ingredient, with its vibrant color and tangy flavor, invites you to experiment with a variety of recipes from classic pies and crumbles to savory main courses and refreshing beverages. With a bit of encouragement and guidance, you can harness the unique qualities of rhubarb to create memorable meals and treats for yourself and your loved ones.

For those who relish the idea of baking, rhubarb desserts offer an exciting playground. Picture a warm rhubarb pie emerging from the oven, its golden crust encasing a sweet tart filling that tantalizes the taste buds. Alternatively, consider a rhubarb crumble, where the fruit's natural acidity is beautifully balanced by a crumbly topping. Even cakes featuring rhubarb can surprise and delight, bringing a refreshing twist to traditional dessert recipes. These treats are not only delicious but also a wonderful way to share the joy of baking with family and friends, making them ideal for gatherings or quiet evenings at home.

Savory dishes are another avenue where rhubarb shines, often taking center stage in unexpected ways. By integrating rhubarb into main courses or side dishes, you can add a layer of depth and complexity to your meals. The tartness of rhubarb pairs well with proteins such as pork or chicken, while its brightness can enhance vegetable medleys. Explore combinations with seasonal produce to create vibrant, healthful dishes that showcase the versatility of this unique ingredient. Experimenting with savory rhubarb recipes can not only diversify your cooking skills but also ignite your passion for creating bold flavors.

Beyond traditional cooking, rhubarb can also be transformed into delightful beverages. From cocktails to smoothies, the tartness of rhubarb adds an invigorating element to drinks, making them perfect for any occasion. A rhubarb infused cocktail can be a refreshing addition to a summer gathering, while a warm rhubarb tea can provide comfort on a chilly evening. These beverages not only highlight rhubarb's unique flavor but also encourage you to think outside the box, inspiring your mixology skills and allowing you to impress guests with creative concoctions.

Finally, embracing rhubarb extends beyond the kitchen; it invites you into the world of preserves and canning. Making rhubarb jams and preserves is a rewarding process that not only enhances your cooking repertoire but also allows you to savor the flavors of rhubarb long after the growing season has passed. This is an excellent opportunity for home cooks to engage in a hands on activity that yields delicious results, perfect for spreading on toast or gifting to friends. With these varied approaches to cooking with rhubarb, you are encouraged to explore, experiment, and enjoy the process, ultimately mastering the art of cooking with this extraordinary ingredient.

Printed in Great Britain
by Amazon